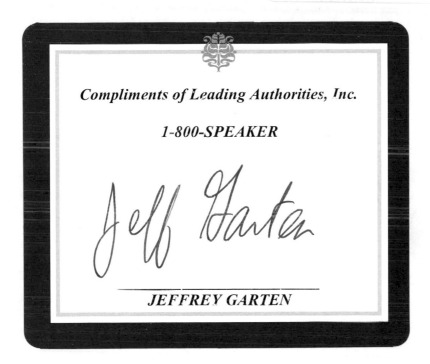

Compliments of Leading Authorities, Inc.

1-800-SPEAKER

JEFFREY GARTEN

The

POLITICS

of

FORTUNE

The

POLITICS

of

FORTUNE

A NEW AGENDA FOR
BUSINESS LEADERS

JEFFREY E. GARTEN

HARVARD BUSINESS SCHOOL PRESS

BOSTON, MASSACHUSETTS

Printed in the United States of America
06 05 04 03 02   5 4 3 2 1

Requests for permission to use or reproduce material from this book should be directed to permissions@hbsp.harvard.edu, or mailed to Permissions, Harvard Business School Publishing, 60 Harvard Way, Boston, Massachusetts 02163.

Library of Congress Cataloging-in-Publication Data

Garten, Jeffrey E., 1946–
The politics of fortune : a new agenda for business leaders /
Jeffrey E. Garten.
p. cm.
Includes bibliographical references and index.
ISBN 1-57851-878-4 (alk. paper)
1. Leadership. 2. Chief executive officers—Attitudes.
3. Executive ability. 4. Business ethics. 5. Social responsibility of business.
6. Corporations—Moral and ethical aspects. 7. International trade—Moral
and ethical aspects. 8. Industrial management—Moral and ethical
aspects. 9. Business and politics—Moral and ethical aspects.
10. Industries—Security measures. 11. National security—United States.
I. Title.
HD57.7 .G377 2002
658.4'08—dc21
2002008472

The paper used in this publication meets the requirements of the American National Standard for Permanence of Paper for Publications and Documents in Libraries and Archives Z39.48–1992.

FOR

INA,

THE CENTER OF MY LIFE

FOR THIRTY-FIVE YEARS

CONTENTS

ACKNOWLEDGMENTS

THIS BOOK WAS WRITTEN as events were unfolding, and everyone involved was extraordinarily gracious under the pressure of a tight schedule. I am deeply indebted to Sara Lippincott, a freelance editor; to Kirsten Sandberg, my editor at the Harvard Business School Press; and to the rest of the superb team at HBSP, including Amanda Elkin, Erin Korey, and Julie Devoll, for all the help they provided on this book. Thanks as well to Rafe Sagalyn, my longtime agent. Will Walker, my assistant, did a wonderful job in helping me to obtain background documents from a wide variety of sources under great time pressure. Mary Ann Green produced one draft after another, working long nights and weekends—as she did with two of my previous books. There is simply no way I can express enough gratitude for her extraordinary competence, good cheer, and endurance.

New Haven, Connecticut
July 2002

CHAPTER 1

A NEW WORLD

A S THE DEAN of a business school, I spend most of my time thinking about how to educate future business leaders. I find it impossible to separate the challenge of identifying the skills and values that our students will need from our judgments about the world in which they will live and work. Their universe will differ substantially from the golden age of capitalism that the United States has enjoyed since the 1980s. Two events in particular have fundamentally altered the landscape: First, the terrorist attacks on the United States on September 11, 2001, exposed a national security problem that is spilling over into every aspect of our lives and will have a pervasive impact on the functioning of the economy as well. Two months later, the scandal involving Enron Corp. and Arthur Andersen LLP, and all the corporate transgressions that were exposed in its wake, severely undermined the integrity of American capitalism.

Each of these events creates new risks for business. Terrorism, by definition, endangers the lives of employees, the security of facilities, and the reliability of operations. What's more, the need to step up safety measures increases the uncertainty about the cost of doing business. The Enron-Andersen debacle has ushered in a period of intense scrutiny of corporate America by lawmakers, investors, and the media, putting extensive new pressures on CEOs, their boards of directors, regulators, accountants, and credit-rating agencies. Together, terrorism and Enron-Andersen challenge the viability of an open society supported by increasingly deregulated markets because they diminish the bonds of trust on which such a free society ultimately depends.

Not surprisingly, the terrorist attacks and the allegations of misbehavior on the part of so much of corporate America have summoned significant government involvement in the economy and beyond, raising profound questions about the extent of Washington's reach. Quite possibly, an excess of regulation will prevent the business community from expanding its range of products and services or otherwise exploiting dynamic market forces. This regulatory excess could jeopardize not only company profits but also economic growth. After almost thirty years of rising political influence, moreover, business leaders could be marginalized as government reemerges as the principal guardian of the nation's welfare. As they were at the end of the nineteenth century, the country's chief executives may well be seen as little more than self-serving protectors of their own special interests.

The U.S. government could initiate policies with good intentions but with unintended consequences, raising the cost of doing business and undercutting opportunities for risk and innovation. What begins as a necessary effort to gather information on suspected terrorists and to monitor their movements ultimately threatens personal privacy and civil liberties. An attempt to adequately fund national security could eventually squeeze other programs vital to the growth of the nation and the economic security of its citizens. The need to impose controls on how people transfer funds or travel internationally—controls implemented to catch terrorists—could slow global commerce and impede immigration. America's current efforts to strengthen the international coalition against terrorism could precipitate a global preoccupation with national security, retarding the global trend toward economic expansion and individual freedom. Regarding the Enron-Andersen scandals—and those that followed, such as WorldCom, Inc.—no one will deny the egregious breaches of law and integrity they entail. Nevertheless, if new regulation doesn't consider the complexities of today's financial markets, then it could result in a regulatory maze that hobbles new investment in the economy, slowing national growth and all that accompanies it—jobs, new technologies, and community development.

Having spent much of my career in the Nixon, Ford, Carter, and Clinton administrations, I have no ideological bias against government. On the contrary, I believe in effective public-sector action when national security is at stake or when markets break down. Indeed, I think that a shift in the balance between regulation and free markets to favor the former is overdue after the free-for-all of the last two decades when the United States unjustifiably deified free markets and vilified government. But now it is possible that Washington could go too far.

We can all appreciate the pressure on Washington to act decisively. After all, what could press a government more than threats to the lives of its citizens and deep flaws in the markets that underlie its economy? But we must recognize that the government is moving into uncharted territory. The struggle to protect ourselves against terror at home—to build ramparts against the vulnerabilities of the world's most open society—could reach every aspect of Americans' lives. We've witnessed big financial collapses before, such as those of Drexel Burnham Lambert Group Inc. in 1990 and Long-Term Capital Management in 1998. However, although some of these debacles involved issues of personal integrity, conflicts of interest, and lack of transparency, none raised such fundamental questions about the American system of accounting and auditing, or the structure of corporate governance that supports American capitalism.

The problem? Once government intervenes, the new rules are difficult to repeal, and a kind of permanent ratcheting-up ensues. For all the talk about the end of the Great Society and big government, we've little evidence of the government's narrowing role in the economy, whether we measure the percentage of taxes relative to the gross domestic product (GDP), the volume and complexity of regulation, or the clout that Washington can exercise at will in the private sector. Indeed, the twentieth century shows that after great international upheavals—World War I, the Great Depression, and World War II—the government extended its reach and rarely retreated. In 1987, *The Economist* conducted a survey of government activity in advanced economies. It made this point:

> Did somebody say the age of big government was dead? At the beginning of this century government spending in today's industrial countries accounted for less than one-tenth of national income. Last year, in the same countries, the government's share of output was roughly half. [In the United States, it went from 3 percent to 33 percent.] Decade by decade, the change in the government's share of the economy moved in one direction only: up.[1]

In this context, we should be especially vigilant after September 11 and Enron. In particular, America and the rest of the world now face a potential reversal of the important momentum toward more political freedom and economic openness that accelerated after the collapse of the Berlin Wall in 1989. If we don't appropriately fine-tune the balance between private and public power, then we'll jeopardize deregulation, the privatization of state-owned companies, and the free movement of capital, goods, services, people, and ideas across borders. We will never be able to calculate the cost of those lost opportunities. How can we measure any decline in the entrepreneurial spirit in America—on products and services that we'll never enjoy, or the talent and energy that we'll never unleash? Even more unquantifiable would

be the costs incurred overseas if there is a slowdown in the opening of markets that have been positively transforming countries
as diverse as China and Mexico, giving hundreds of millions of
citizens a better material life and a freer existence. Most important of all, and most difficult to measure, would be the impact of
more government on individual freedom of action and thought,
on privacy, and on the liberties that so many of us have been for-
tunate enough to have taken for granted.

To use a term popularized by Andrew Grove, the chairman of Intel
Corporation, the United States is at a "strategic inflection point"
—a moment when the basis for strategy changes, requiring a fundamental course correction. In his 1996 book, *Only the Paranoid
Survive,* Grove lists several strategic inflection points in the business world. He describes how Japanese memory-chip producers
nearly destroyed Intel in the mid-1980s by bringing new technologies and new strategies to compete with U.S. firms. Had Intel
not moved into the field of microprocessors just at the dawn of the
age of personal computers, the firm could have collapsed. Grove
emphasized the powerful forces of change that were at work.[2]

But strategic inflection points occur not only in the business
world. They also occur as a result of disruptions in a nation's political, economic, and social climate. The 1930s depression, the
Japanese bombing of Pearl Harbor, the first explosion of the atomic
bomb, the opening of China, and the collapse of the Berlin Wall
are obvious examples. Regardless of the current direction of the
United States, September 11, 2001, and the Enron-Andersen
fallout constitute powerful strategic inflection points. Alone, either would easily qualify as being a critical discontinuity in our
lives. But, for many reasons, their combined effect on the balance between government and business could constitute an earth-
quake in American society.

Think of America at the beginning of 2000: Before the terror-ist attacks and Enron's collapse, markets—and not the government —were ascendant. The domestic and international economies were fast becoming "frictionless." Businesses were honing their operations with ever-slimmer inventories, just-in-time deliver-ies, and global supply chains that exploited the most efficient manufacturers in every part of the world. At home, Americans were increasingly entrusting their fate to the stock market, and this so-called equity culture was spreading from Buenos Aires to Beijing. Jack Welch, then chairman and CEO of the General Electric Company, and John Chambers, CEO of Cisco Systems, Inc., were heroes and icons, as were their corporate counterparts overseas. Enron was among the world's most admired compa-nies. Deregulation was a driving force in America and most other nations. The push to increase the connections between coun-tries by lowering barriers to trade and investment—the push for more globalization—was at the center of American foreign policy and international politics. National borders were fading. More-over, most top government officials and CEOs assumed that an era of peace and prosperity was at hand, and that American-style capitalism was the most acceptable model.

This snapshot of 2000 is enough to show how much has changed. Today, business is hunkering down, focusing less on dramatic innovation than on the accuracy of its financial state-ments. There are virtually no CEOs in the category of hero. "Business leaders are being knocked off their pedestals faster than the Communist heroes after the fall of the Berlin Wall," wrote *The Economist* in late spring of 2002.[3] "Across the busi-ness landscape, the imperial chief executive, hailed not long ago as the savior of entire companies and the driving force behind the turnaround of the American economy, is suddenly under seige," wrote David Leonhardt in the *New York Times* in the summer.[4] Equally important, an increasing amount of sand has collected in the gears of the U.S. and global economy; doing business has become considerably more expensive. In February 2002, *Fortune* projected that, in the year following September 11, 2001, American companies could spend the following incremental amounts on security: $65 billion on logistics, $35 billion on insurance and liability, $18 billion on workplace security, $15 billion on safeguarding information technology, and $12 billion on added costs for travel and transportation.[5] These expenses, amounting to almost $150 billion in the year after the attacks, constitute 1.5 percent of GDP and include property insurance, workers' compensation, higher rent for buildings in which the latest security equipment has been installed, enhanced Internet security, travel delays, and so forth. This estimate does not include the psychological impact on executives and employees operating in a more fragile environment. David Wyss, chief economist for Standard & Poor's, says corporate America will pay an incremental $135 billion for homeland security in 2002 (including $20 billion for workplace security, $15 billion for back-up information systems, and $35 billion for higher insurance premiums). David Hale, chief global economist for Zurich Financial Services Group, estimates security spending will reduce corporate profits in 2002 by 5 to 6 percent.[6] And, of course, these projected costs pale in comparison with the effect that another terrorist attack would have on business.

There are other costs to business that have not yet come into clear focus. If security concerns result in companies holding higher inventories, the price tag could be large. If the uncertain security environment in many developing countries results in a slowdown in foreign direct investment, as may well be the case, then global trade will slow. The combined impact of terrorism and the "Enron effect" could also tarnish the American market for foreign investors. Because the United States borrows over $1 billion a day from abroad to finance its trade deficit, a slowdown in foreign investment could cause a number of painful adjustments. The combination of terrorism and corporate malfeasance could also cast a pall on stock markets for more than just a few quarters. This situation certainly existed in the spring and early summer of 2002, and to the extent it continues, the value of companies in many key sectors could be vastly reduced, raising the cost of financing for them, slowing their new investments, and retarding the growth of the U.S. and world economies.

But neither the increased cost of doing business nor the impact on the economy should be our greatest worry. Depending on the full ramifications of the response to terrorism and the Enron-Andersen debacle—something we won't know for a few years—these two milestones could shake our faith in the viability of an open society of the kind that Americans have known—a society in which ideas flow freely; civil liberties and privacy are protected; markets are free to generate products, services, and wealth; and government intrusion is kept to the bare minimum. Our greater fear? That these features of life will gradually erode. Indeed, the erosion may already be happening. Government is back. Borders are back. Serious military conflicts are escalating around the world, and the United States may be entering a period when national security is an all-encompassing preoccupation. Globalization has become a double-edged sword: It facilitates not only trade across borders but also heinous crime. And the many transgressions in the corporate world have tarnished the American model of capitalism, with implications for everything from our basic freedoms to the position of the United States in the world.

A continuation of the progress and prosperity of the last two decades of the twentieth century depends on defining the proper relationship between the private and the public sectors. There is some irony to this challenge. Considering the headlines of the 1980s and 1990s, the number of cover stories that depicted CEOs as heroes, and the free-market rhetoric from both Washington and corporate America, someone might think that the United States had entered an era in which business drove the economic boom without government help. The fact is, though, that the interplay between the private and the public sector largely fostered that prosperity. After all, the government invented the Internet and allowed its commercialization. The monetary policies of the Federal Reserve, the fiscal policies of the U.S. Treasury, and the free-trade stance of the Clinton administration all contributed to low inflation and budget surpluses in the late 1990s, the heart of the long business expansion. Legislation allowed deregulation in finance, transportation, and telecommunications (imperfect as it may have been). Moreover, government-negotiated treaties led to expanded trade. That's why we must get the balance between government and business right.

The United States does not have a lot of maneuvering room in managing its sophisticated economy. True, American companies have grown larger, more powerful, more globally focused, and more technologically complex. As noted, government has also grown steadily. Yet, amid both trends, the nation has become more fragile. We saw how the destruction of just two large skyscrapers affected the U.S. and global economies, and now everyone sees how much greater the damage will be if someone attacks other parts of the nation's critical infrastructure—energy grids, telecommunications centers, food supplies, and the like. Quite separately, but almost simultaneously, we saw how quickly major companies with excellent reputations—Enron and Arthur Andersen—can collapse, and how fast other corporate icons such as General Electric and Merrill Lynch & Co., Inc. can lose their market value when facing intense public scrutiny. There are several reasons for this fragility: One is the interlocking nature of all aspects of modern society. Another is the growing demand for transparency in American institutions. There is the instant global reach of the media, and a growing skepticism among ordinary citizens that most big institutions, public and private, can be trusted. One inevitable conclusion is that neither business nor government alone can shore up the overall system. It will take both, working together.

This partnership becomes critical when you put American society in a global context. In the international economy, in which instability is particularly great, there are few rules and institutions. Developing them will take many decades. National governments and business leaders are poorly equipped for the job. Both can abdicate, in which case there will be anarchy. Or they can cooperate to build truly international institutions, in which case the world has a better chance to enjoy a smoothly functioning global economy.

The United States has a lot to do, and neither Washington nor corporate America can do it alone. Over the next several years, the antiterrorism campaign and the response to Enron will result, one way or another, in the rewriting of the rules that govern so much of business and society. How free will Americans be to move around? How much privacy will they sacrifice? What restrictions will the United States place on finance, trade, immigration, communications? How will corporate governance change? How can a nation wage war and live in peace and prosperity at the same time? Someone will make decisions on these and a host of related issues. The question is, Who and how?

Americans need no less than a new paradigm for leadership in their society. In this book, I am looking at the agenda for business leaders, but, of course, they constitute just one important element of a more complicated picture. I don't know precisely what this paradigm should be, but I know that the roles of business, government, and nongovernmental organizations must move in the direction of closer partnership. They must coalesce around a vision of a society in which many new security measures will be taken, yet be carefully weighed against the freedoms that the United States defends. Leaders across sectors must construe security in not just military terms but economic ones. They must understand that global problems are increasingly inseparable from what happens at home. For business leaders in particular, the new paradigm of leadership must go beyond pleasing Wall Street and delivering ever higher profits on a quarterly basis. Besides considering all the stakeholders of a company—employees, customers, suppliers, communities—business leaders must also consider the concerns of society, such as a cleaner environment and a higher level of integrity in business dealings.

Indeed, business and other leaders must rethink how they can collaborate to further the public interest on a range of critical issues. I know that a definition of the "public interest" is elusive, but let me explain what I have in mind. First of all, the public interest is not simply the sum of the private interests, which are often self-serving and short-term. Nor is a market economy the same as a market society; prices and competition should not govern everything. Moreover, in a highly sophisticated, market-oriented nation such as the United States, the public interest cannot be defined by democratic voting alone or by the judgment of officials responding to opinion polls. American society is more complicated than that. It needs interest groups; it needs political parties. And, given the powerful role that business plays in U.S. society, the nation needs a level of leadership from corporate America that goes beyond that of an interest group and looks at public policy from a more strategic perspective. It needs chief executives who can explain to the government and the public the effects of various policies on the economy over the long term, the risks and rewards of different policy choices, and whom these policies will affect. It needs leaders who can look at the overall economic system and examine ways to strengthen it and recommend national and international policies that will expand open markets and promote democracy—two conditions that reinforce each another. It needs business executives, too, who can expose and condemn the business practices that undermine effective capitalism.

All this translates not into a business community off to the side pursuing its own agenda, or one that sees itself in opposition to government, but one characterized by a closer partnership with government. Such a partnership will bring a market-oriented approach to complex policy decisions and will help guarantee that the nation uses the initiative, resources, and talents of the private sector whenever possible. This approach not only avoids unnecessary expansion of the state but also enhances the government's effectiveness when it does intervene.

In centering my attention on business-government ties, I do not mean that the leaders of corporations should occupy a privileged position in society or in policy development to the exclusion of other groups such as public interest organizations, professional associations, representatives of labor, and educators. At this moment in history, however, business leadership in particular needs attention, and the potential for a more constructive leadership role for corporate America is especially large. In the end, however, the country needs the most inclusive partnerships it can muster, including business-government alliances, but going well beyond that.

When you think about the most important questions before the country, almost every question requires a coordinated public and private sector response. The policy and management systems needed in the years ahead do not yet exist; they have to evolve now, and quickly. To bring this about, the United States will need the combined talents, resources, and management techniques of the public and private sectors.

Numerous challenges compel stronger business-government ties in the public policy arena. First, the United States must protect its critical infrastructure from attack. This means shielding its systems for communication, transportation, energy, water, and public health. The nation must know what measures to take, who should take them, and who should pay for them. It must determine how to minimize the increased business costs of antiterrorism measures—protection of software and facilities, higher insurance premiums, longer and more expensive travel delays, and the like. But because so much of the country's infrastructure is in private hands, only a new model for a business-government partnership will work.

Second, the spate of corporate scandals requires an extensive analysis of what went wrong, who was responsible, and how to fix the system. The combined investigations by Congress and the Securities and Exchange Commission, as well as the actions of state attorneys general and possibly a few business groups, may address many specific transgressions. There is a risk of overreaction, but there is also a risk that many important issues will disappear in another economic boom when attention is turned elsewhere. Both overreaction and public indifference would be a mistake. The nation needs a careful postmortem that encompasses a deep-seated examination of America's business culture. Among the issues to be examined are the relative merits of government regulation and self-regulation, the best type of compensation systems to align a company's management with the long-term interests of shareholders and other stakeholders, ways to prevent conflicts of interest from undercutting market integrity, and ways to promote honesty and trust within companies and between them and their constituencies. A joint business-government effort to reexamine the basics of America's business environment will resonate more than an effort by either entity alone.

A third challenge is that as the nation returns to an era of budget deficits, it must find ways to preserve the social safety net, including programs for health care, Social Security, and privately financed pensions. The problem of financing is monumental, given the competing priorities of national defense at home and abroad. Because business helps fund the social programs, which affect the morale and productivity of the national work force, and because the costs of these programs will be rising, the public and private sectors should design solutions together.

Another principal challenge for policy makers in the global economy is to maintain the momentum for expanded trade and investment. This challenge occurs precisely when security concerns are producing new restrictions, the marketplace is becoming more fragmented by region and level of income, and antiglobal protests are fueling a political backlash against continued economic liberalization. We cannot take for granted that globalization, as we have known it, will proceed smoothly; in fact, we should assume that it will not. New rules and institutions will all require a greater level of cooperation between business and government leaders.

Developed and developing nations also face the task of lifting billions of people out of poverty. This constitutes a fifth challenge for business and government leaders. For several decades, the United States and industrialized countries have given little more than lip service to providing effective help for poor countries. Without a tangible and substantial commitment now—without new approaches to trade, aid, education, and public health, all requiring new business-government partnerships, as well as partnerships with nongovernmental organizations—we will be turning our backs on the great moral issue of our times. And in this interconnected world, we can expect the frustrations of the poor to end in violence and on our own doorsteps. This is especially true when dealing with many Islamic countries, with their dim political and economic prospects.

Sixth, the role of global corporations as "citizens" in countries and communities around the world is sparking intense controversy. As companies face challenges for which there are no consistent global laws or concrete standards—challenges relating to the environment, labor, business practices, corporate roles in education, and human rights—they must balance their fiduciary responsibility to shareholders in a highly competitive marketplace with considerations that include their own corporate and moral values, their roles in strengthening the society around them, and the rewards and risks to their reputation. The issues are horrendously complex, and virtually no CEO is trained to handle them. But one thing is certain: To make the best judgments, companies must develop cooperative strategies with home and host governments, international institutions, and nongovernmental organizations.

Next, radical changes in the scope and direction of U.S. foreign policy could destabilize the environment for global business. The disproportionate military and economic power of the United States is now on full display, creating deep anxiety around the world. While using the rhetoric of multilateral cooperation, the United States is behaving as though it needed no one else. Even America's closest allies—England, Canada, Germany, and Japan —are deeply worried about U.S. unilateralism. Meanwhile, Washington, in its preoccupation with terrorism, is according priority to military-to-military and international intelligence relationships and forging links to repressive regimes that represent the opposite of the values that support liberal democratic capitalism. Because much of American foreign policy could undermine global business, the nation needs much closer synchronization of national security and business goals and requirements.

Finally, a new paradigm for business leadership requires rethinking the basics of business education. We must equip CEOs to manage their companies for short-term profitability but also for long-term value. They must learn to focus not only on the internal efficiencies of their companies but also on the external relationships and policies—including interaction with governments, international institutions, and nongovernmental organizations. Business executives must understand better their overall responsibilities when it comes to the systems, values, and culture that drive their global enterprises. But just as war cannot be left entirely to the generals, the rethinking of business education is too important to be left to the business establishment. The task of improving business education ought to include leaders from the worlds of government, labor, science, academia, and foundations.

In short, the agenda for business leaders working in cooperation with government and often with nongovernmental organizations is nothing short of formidable.

CHAPTER 2

PRECEDENTS FOR

LEADERSHIP

G O BACK to the early 1940s. The United States had just entered World War II, and the economy was on a wartime footing. America's industrial plants had been converted for military production. Rationing and price controls were imposed, too. CEOs were de facto draftees; they became part of the effort to mobilize for the military battles ahead.

But large problems loomed. Millions of soldiers (the number eventually reached 19 million) would be demobilized into a peacetime economy, and government and corporate planners feared that not enough jobs would be available. The formative experience of most business leaders and policy makers had been the 1930s depression, which included the isolationism and economic protectionism that characterized the period. The leaders' major concern was to avoid falling into that trap again. "There are a lot of changes we've got to make in our economic thinking to prevent a depression," said Robert Nathan, a prominent economist of the time. "If nothing is done to stabilize the economy and get high employment [after the war], then we are going to have a depression that will shake the free enterprise system to the ground."[1]

Amid this set of difficult circumstances, Paul G. Hoffman, then president of Studebaker Corporation; William Benton, cofounder of Benton & Bowles advertising agency; and Marion B. Folsom, treasurer of Eastman Kodak Company, founded the Committee for Economic Development (CED) in 1942. Hoffman served as chairman. At the beginning the committee had about twenty members (or trustees, as they were called), all business leaders, both Democrats and Republicans. Among them were Thomas McCabe, CEO of Scott Paper; Henry Luce of *Time, Life,* and *Fortune*; Marshall Field, head of the retailing empire; and Beardsley Ruml, treasurer of R. H. Macy Company. Launched with the strong encouragement of Secretary of Commerce Jesse Jones, the group looked to organize and present business views on how the United States could make the transition to a peacetime economy and beyond.[2]

The CED wasn't launched without a substantial amount of behind-the-scenes struggles among various factions in the business world, not to mention doubts within the U.S. government itself. Business-government relationships had had a tortuous history over the previous century. After the Civil War, American companies expanded across the country with minimal government interference. But by the beginning of the twentieth century, Washington, led by President Theodore Roosevelt, began to exert countervailing regulatory pressure. During the 1930s President Franklin Roosevelt expanded government's reach over the private sector, with bitter reaction from most of the business community. By the beginning of World War II, many CEOs had accumulated substantial experience both in fighting the government and in cooperating with it.

As the historian Karl Schriftgiesser notes in his definitive history of the CED, *Business Comes of Age,* much of the U.S. business community of the early 1940s subscribed to the pithy economic philosophy of an anonymous late-nineteenth-century sage: "Self, self, self is the axiom of evolution, the postulate of political economy, the rule of human action."[3] Most business leaders harbored a deep suspicion of Washington, especially after the expansion of government in the New Deal. Several mavericks, however, studied the steady rise in government activism since the turn of the century and the consequent intertwining of the economy with the public sector. Interested in the survival of private enterprise, these men realized that it could thrive only in a mixed economy.

As it happened, their thinking was matched by the secretary of commerce, Texas politician and businessman Jesse Jones. Though a conservative, Jones was interested in solving problems, not fighting them. He understood that America's postwar economic viability rested heavily not just on a resumption of production and trade but on a marked increase in each. For that, there would have to be closer collaboration between the public and private sectors than what most CEOs or top government officials had ever envisioned. Jones hosted meetings of business executives, and he even helped choose the initial group of CED leaders, calling for a permanent committee of "outstanding business authorities who are also public-spirited citizens."[4] With them, he agreed that the new organization would be independent of the government, that its work would be based on impartial and independent research, and that its mandate would be to help chart the nation's economic policies once the cataclysm of World War II was over.

The CED initially searched for policies that would get the nation to sustainable full employment within a free-enterprise framework. At that time, it appeared all too likely that the government would continue to play the overwhelming role it had assumed in wartime. The CED was pragmatic enough not to embrace an extreme free-market model, given that substantial support from Washington would be essential during the transition. The group's research was undertaken by some of the nation's best economic experts (including John Kenneth Galbraith, a liberal, and Herbert Stein, a conservative), who worked closely with business leaders.

From the late 1940s through the mid-1960s, the CED wielded significant influence in the United States through the policy analysis and recommendations it issued. The committee described its mission as carrying out research "without regard to and independently of the special interests of any group in the body politic, either political, social, or economic."[5] Its work was widely read in the government and discussed in the media. Its reports dealt with fundamental problems that politicians had trouble coming to grips with. Topics ran the gamut of the critical questions of the day: how price controls should be gradually dismantled; what system of taxation would provide enough revenue to keep the government's budgets in balance; the relationship between fiscal and monetary policies in the postwar period; the management of the federal debt; urban renewal; the revitalization of federalism; and the improvement of the government's management practices.

The reports were nonideological and often more centrist than readers expected from a business group. They contained the dissents of individual members, so that the public could see the full range of views. Nor was the CED averse to disagreeing with other business groups, such as the U.S. Chamber of Commerce or the National Association of Manufacturers, both of which saw themselves as advocates for their members' needs and often took sharply partisan positions. Among the CED's recommendations were support for tax cuts and spending to expand the postwar economy. The committee endorsed government planning for the prevention of unemployment. In contrast to many other business organizations, the CED supported the labor movement. It was an enthusiastic proponent of economic help to Europe and elsewhere, for the revival of markets for American exports. The committee also helped lay the groundwork for the International Monetary Fund and The World Bank.

The quality of its members also gave the CED clout. Many of them had established reputations in both business and public service during Roosevelt's New Deal. Many later went on to serve in the Truman and Eisenhower administrations as ambassadors, as senior presidential advisers, or in cabinet posts. They were a special breed of business leader, tempered by the depression and war and experienced in the culture of government. For the most part, these men were centrists, steering the line between the values of the New Deal and the radical right, between socialism and unrestrained laissez-faire.

Here is another example of how American business leaders played a highly influential role in forming government policies. On January 5, 1947, in an address at Harvard University, Secretary of State George Marshall proposed a far-reaching plan for the recovery of Europe from wartime devastation. He reasoned that a prostrate Continent could not recover on its own. Market forces alone would not suffice, and without considerable American help, Secretary Marshall said, Europe would face "economic, social, and political deterioration of a very grave order."[6] He believed that this state of affairs would do serious damage to U.S. economic interests, since the United States would lose critical market for its exports.

The Marshall Plan became the foundation for U.S. foreign and trade policy as it unfolded during the Cold War. Billions of

U.S. dollars and tons of U.S. products crossed the Atlantic in what was the most significant act of international economic cooperation and the most clear-cut synthesis of altruism and self-interest ever attempted. Today, the success of the Marshall Plan remains one of America's and Europe's greatest achievements. Integral to the plan was substantial participation by the U.S. and European private sectors.[7]

American business leaders participated at almost every level. Among the main channels of business activity was the Economic Cooperation Administration (ECA), established in 1948 as the hub in an elaborate network of public-private power sharing. Its members read like a *Who's Who* of business: James Zellerbach, chairman of Crown Zellerbach Corporation; George W. Merck, chairman of Merck & Co.; Clarence Randall of the Inland Steel Corporation; Cecil Burrill of the Standard Oil Company of N.J.; Charles Wilson of the General Motors Corporation; John McCaffrey of International Harvester; W. Averell Harriman of Brown Brothers Harriman; Joseph Dodge of the Detroit Bank (Dodge would eventually play a major role in the reconstruction of Japan)—to name but a few. The ECA was proposed by the Truman administration and created by congressional legislation. Its purpose was to work with the European private sector to revive Europe's economies—to restart industrial and agricultural production, open distribution and trading channels, and arrange credit. The ECA worked hand in glove with the Departments of State, Treasury, and Agriculture. It established industry councils in the United States to support its work and encouraged joint industry councils across the Atlantic. The goal was not just to generate economic activity, critical as that was, but also to promote private-sector initiative and innovation and to introduce American management techniques. The ECA organized technical assistance programs and conferences and worked to build a transnational business network based on public-private collaboration. It made an invaluable contribution to the overall success of the Marshall Plan.

I am not proposing carbon copies of the major policy-influencing business institutions of the 1940s. Obviously, the times are very different. But the two eras share some features. In both cases, business and government leaders are confronted with a changing industrial structure combined with a new set of geopolitical circumstances. Now, as then, business and government leaders need each another; they certainly have little to gain from not cooperating. In both cases, CEOs hold a critical role in the shaping of public policy that aims to promote economic development.

Moreover, some features of the CED and ECA would serve chief executives and the nation well if put in place today. The most important aspect of both the organizations is that they rose above the interests of any one firm or industry and focused instead on the public interest through a pragmatic business lens. At a time when there was no shortage of political debate at home, the CED and ECA tried to advance ideas that were based on thoughtful research and that could translate into workable policies and programs. The ECA, in particular, brought modern management techniques to the implementation of complex policies. In their capacity as institutions, neither the CED nor the ECA were involved in campaign contributions of any kind. They did not endorse political candidates. Neither saw itself as a lobbying group, except insofar as it wanted to advance broad ideas and policy choices that the government should consider.

To put it another way, business can have at least four types of relationships with government: First, business might consider government as the enemy—a force in opposition to its interests.

Second, it might think of government as a source of handouts—
a big sugar daddy. Third, business and government could form
partnerships to promote a variety of projects—education, space
travel, health research, urban development, transportation systems, economic development in the Third World. And fourth,
business and government could form a strategic partnership
based on a common desire to chart the future course for the
nation. The hallmark of the CED and ECA lies in some combination of the third and fourth relationships.

If the participation of CEOs is to be constructive and quali-
tatively different from what now exists, however, they must re-
capture at least the spirit of the CED and the ECA. When we
look ahead to the kinds of roles that business leaders might play
in public policy, we see several alternative mechanisms for business leadership:

> ➤ Business associations like the CED that focus not on firms
>   or industries but on broad public-interest issues

> ➤ Specialized advisory boards that interact with government
>   on such questions as homeland security and foreign policy

> ➤ High-powered commissions with substantial CEO represen-
>   tation to examine broad national issues—for example, rebuild-
>   ing integrity in the financial markets, or rethinking the role
>   of management education in a world in which a new relation-
>   ship between public and private interests is required

> ➤ Specific public-private partnerships that marshal the
>   expertise and resources for such matters as cyber-security
>   or development projects in the Islamic world

> ➤ Lobbying groups that push not for specific company inter-
>   ests (although self-motivated lobbying will occur, in any
>   event) but for more effective national and international

responses to challenges, in such arenas as economic
development or foreign policy

I'm not saying that none of this public-private cooperation
exists today. Some business associations place priority on public
policy, although they all fall woefully short in terms of the scope
of their work, their objectivity, and the consistency of their efforts. The CED survives, although with much-diminished clout.
The National Planning Association produces interesting policy
papers, but it, too, is a pale reflection of what the nation requires. Although the Council on Competitiveness does excellent
work, its focus is relatively limited to one subject: American
competitiveness. The Concord Coalition likewise deals with
one issue: fiscal policy. The Business Roundtable, comprising
over one hundred active CEOs of the top U.S. companies, has
taken some important stands on trade and education, but many
of its positions are narrowly based on the interests of its members, as opposed to the public interest. Moreover, its work is
often not supported by the kind of research that characterized
the original CED. Public-private efforts also arise in everything
from urban development projects to information technology.
There is no lack of advisory boards and commissions. However,
I am arguing for a different order of magnitude—a higher level
of effectiveness and influence by business leadership—and the
public's acceptance of a rebalanced relationship between business and government. In all these areas, there is substantial
room for improvement.

Could it happen? Could the U.S. business community recap-
ture the collective spirit that existed among some of its prede-
cessors in the late 1940s? I believe that it can. The American
political and economic system can be highly responsive to

changing circumstances; indeed, this pragmatic flexibility is one of its great strengths. Americans have been able to maintain a vibrant democracy and a vigorous market economy through different stages of the nation's economic development—through booms and busts, through war and peace, and through Republican and Democratic presidential administrations and Congresses. Socialism has never been a serious threat, nor has right-wing authoritarianism. These historical patterns put the United States in a unique category among countries.

A strong argument can be made that September 11, 2001, has changed the environment in which business leaders will now operate—indeed, that the terrorist attacks have changed society's expectation of what leaders can be. I also believe that the Enron debacle was the culmination of a long era of personal greed and commercial excess, and that the public is ready for the pendulum to swing back to more fundamental and traditional values. Americans may well have entered a period in which the notions of patriotism and community spirit are back in a way not seen since the early days of the Cold War.

In a thoughtful book written in 1982, Albert O. Hirschman, professor of social science at the Institute for Advanced Study, wrote about these themes. He examined the historical cycles of nations as the mood shifted from periods of individualism, self-indulgence, and a general inward-looking mind-set to a focus by citizens on public affairs. He said that an interest in and a yearning for public involvement arise after a long period of personal consumption. The mood swing is usually the result of one or more major crises that shock the country, and of a sense among individuals that consumption alone is no longer satisfying enough. Thus the boom of the 1920s in the United States was interrupted by the 1929 stock market crash and the depression, and led to an active citizen involvement in public policy in the 1930s and an even more heightened interest once World War II began. The long economic boom during the 1960s, a period of considerable self-indulgence, was interrupted by Vietnam and ushered in another period of public consciousness, reflected in mass movements for consumer protection, environmental protection, and gender equality.[8]

Historian Arthur M. Schlesinger Jr. described the same pattern. In *The Cycles of American History,* he describes how "affirmative" government and "public-purpose" presidential administrations have regularly emerged to steady markets after a frenzy of laissez-faire policies. "The tradition of affirmative government is quite as authentically American, quite as deeply ingrained in our national history, quite as strongly identified with our greatest statesmen, quite as expressive of American ideas and character, as the competing tradition of self-interest and scrambling private enterprise," he wrote.[9]

There are good reasons to believe that Americans are now ready to pay more attention to issues of public interest. In the 1990s, the stock market was the barometer of national health, and many people seemed willing to trust free markets rather than government when it came to the national welfare. "The 1980s was a decade of greed and excess, and by the end of it people were feeling fairly disgusted with themselves. . . . [Then] the 1990s turned into one of the most repulsively narcissistic decades of modern times," wrote Richard Tompkins in the *Financial Times.* Of the same period, *Time* essayist Roger Rosenblatt put it this way: "America has been hydroplaning on the present, creating and devouring a culture consisting of relentless ephemera."[10] It's possible—even likely—that the first decade of the twenty-first century will reflect a sharp reaction to the 1980s and 1990s and will see the United States move into a more public-spirited age.

Moreover, there is now a sense in the United States—and in the world—that big problems can be solved only when there is collaboration between all major groups directly interested in the solutions. Partnerships of many constituencies are the only way to harness the extraordinary amount of information and the experience available for dealing with the complexities of today's markets. Go-it-alone approaches are out; teamwork is in. As Jack Welch once put it, "the challenge to solving any problem is to get every mind in the game."[11]

The Bush administration, populated as it is with former CEOs—including the president himself, the vice president, the secretary of defense, and the secretary of the treasury—has a chance to capitalize on the new public spirit. The administration's first year in office was spent allowing—even encouraging—business to plead for its selfish interests. But just as September 11 changed other approaches to policy, the president and his top officials can change their ways with regard to the role of business, challenging CEOs to think and act more constructively about the national interest. This impulse will doubtless be reinforced by the need to restore public confidence in the integrity of U.S. markets. Indeed, President Bush has gone a long way toward setting the right tone. "After America was attacked," he told the nation in his State of the Union speech in January 2002, "we were reminded that we are citizens, with obligations to each other, to our country, and to history. We began to think less of the goods we can accumulate, and more about the good we can do." Later on, in a speech to a business audience, he spoke of the importance of responsibility and trust: "America is ushering in a responsibility era, a culture regaining a sense of responsibility . . . and this new culture must include a sense of corporate responsibility. Business relationships, like all human relationships, are built on a foundation of integrity and trust. When those values are practiced and expected, our economy and our country are stronger."[12] These statements are not a bad starting point for what has to happen—and what *can* happen—now.

CHAPTER 3

REBUILDING THE

REPUTATION OF CEOS

W HAT WILL BUSINESS LEADERS NEED to do to play a
more elevated and effective role in public policy? To
begin with, they will have to make a Herculean effort to regain
the public trust that they have lost in the last two years. America
has always had a love-hate relationship with corporations, particularly large ones. Big companies have been a channel for opportunity, upward mobility, and technological progress. In many
communities, they have been a major employer, a pivotal con-
tributor to philanthropic causes, and a powerful force for social
stability. They have given us great rags-to-riches legends and provided many well-known leaders, from Andrew Carnegie to Bill
Gates. But Americans have often mistrusted corporate power,
often equating it with the notion of monopoly and conspiracy.
President Theodore Roosevelt talked about the "malefactors of
great wealth." President Franklin D. Roosevelt railed against
"economic royalists." President Dwight D. Eisenhower warned
against the emergence of a "military-industrial complex." At any
given time, no doubt, some segments of the population admire
CEOs, and some segments resent them, but nowadays the balance seems to be shifting toward the negative.

For one thing, the terrorist attacks of 2001 highlighted government's role as the ultimate protector of the people's personal
security—at the very time that the boom of the 1990s had come
to an end and business leaders appeared far less powerful than
they had during the last two decades. The ensuing collapse of
Enron and all the scandals in its wake raised a number of issues
at the heart of the American business environment: dubious
financial reporting and outright fraud, and lapses in the performance of credit-rating agencies, stock analysts, auditors, government regulators, and boards of directors. The public resented
CEOs whose compensation arrangements insured that they
would bear little risk for financial failure, while their employees,
their company's shareholders, and other constituencies suffered.
Although Enron was an extreme case, these sorts of problems sur-
faced in many other well-known companies, too, such as Global
Crossing, Qwest Communications International, Inc., WorldCom,
Tyco International, Ltd., Xerox Corporation, Adelphia Communications, and ImClone Systems Inc. Even companies such as
General Electric, IBM, and AOL Time Warner were criticized for
the way they had been reporting their financial results. Nor was
the environment of corporate scandal limited to industrial companies; several major Wall Street firms—Merrill Lynch, Salomon
Smith Barney, Morgan Stanley Dean Witter & Co., among them—
were being investigated for allegedly manipulating their research
to make some companies appear stronger than they were, so that
the Wall Street firms could obtain new business from corporate
clients. In May 2002, the cover of *The Economist* contained this
headline: "Fallen Idols: The Overthrow of Celebrity CEOs," with
the lead story describing how the corporate titans of the late
1990s were highly overrated. That same week, the cover of *Business Week* asked, "Wall Street: How Corrupt Is It?" Its lead story
had an answer: "Plenty."[1]

As happens when people take a closer look at any systemic
breakdown, it became evident that corporate behavior had been

deteriorating for a while. In 1998, according to the *New York Times*, a survey of 160 chief financial officers at public companies found that two-thirds had been pressured by their colleagues to misrepresent their financial reports, and 12 percent gave in.[2] In late 2001 a survey of 190 chief financial officers by *CFO* magazine indicated that more than one-fifth of those polled felt that they had misled investors.[3] Another study found that between 1998 and 2000, public companies revised their financial statements 464 times after presenting them to the public—nearly as many times as the 1980s and 1990s combined.[4]

These problems emerged at a time when Americans had begun investing in the stock market as never before, making the financial and political impact of corporate transgressions far more severe than the fallout from previous financial scandals. In the 1990s, the amount of investment in mutual funds reached $4 trillion—sixteen times what it was at the beginning of the decade—and by 2002 about 80 million Americans owned stock either directly or through these funds. The numbers are less significant than the underlying trend. Since the early 1990s, one company after another has been shifting from a "defined-benefit" pension plan to a "defined-contribution" plan—meaning that rather than setting aside money for guaranteed retirement, employees are investing their own funds for retirement. The implication is that with every year that passes, the fate of more and more Americans will be linked to the stock markets.

This kind of linkage between the stock market and the future of so many American citizens is unprecedented in the history of the United States or any other nation. Whatever the public's feeling toward corporations, it has been betting heavily on corporate success—and now it feels betrayed. In a *Business Week* poll conducted in mid-January 2002, only a third of the respondents felt that big companies followed ethical business practices, and just a quarter thought that these firms are honest in dealing with employees and customers. Twenty-four percent had "hardly any" confidence in people running major corporations.[5] On April 12, 2002, a *Wall Street Journal*/NBC poll showed "ominous signs that trust has waned in corporations [and] financial institutions." Fifty-seven percent of the respondents said that the standards and values of corporate leaders have dropped since the 1980s.[6] Not surprisingly, the pace of government investigation of corporate misdeeds accelerated. In the first three months of 2002, the SEC more than doubled the number of investigations it opened compared to the first quarter of 2001.[7] Still, it was the big names in corporate America in such sectors as finance, telecommunications, and energy that set the tone. "Every year we have had progressively more financial fraud cases," Charles Niemeir, head of accounting in the Securities and Exchange Commission's enforcement division, told the *Wall Street Journal*. "[But] the bigger story is the size of the companies being investigated. We are investigating more Fortune 500 companies than we ever have."[8]

Declining confidence in business leaders has not been confined to the United States either. By June 2002, the problem erupted in Europe, with a particular focus on executive compensation—perhaps an easy surrogate for broader public concerns about corporate malfeasance. CEO pay at several European corporate giants has come under intense scrutiny from shareholders and politicians; targets include ABB, Vodafone, Deutsche Telekom, Prudential plc, Vivendi Universal, and Alcatel.[9] In a poll of fourteen European countries conducted by the *Wall Street Journal Europe* and GfK AdHoc Research Worldwide, only 21 percent of respondents said most CEOs are honest, 70 percent said they are paid too much, and 59 percent said governments should step in to regulate CEO salaries.[10]

Then, too, the 1980s and 1990s encouraged the worst sort of government-business collaboration—a type of crony capitalism that Washington so often criticizes in countries like Indonesia and Argentina. Since the days of Ronald Reagan, presidential administrations have been unabashedly business friendly. In working with corporate America to regain its competitiveness against Japan and Germany, in lavishing attention on Silicon Valley, in promoting American exports and investment abroad, in pressing for deregulation and tax reduction at home, in taking a low-key approach to antitrust action, Presidents Reagan, Bush, Clinton, and now George W. Bush were deeply support- ive of their business constituency, almost never requiring any quid pro quo.

For over twenty years a business culture has been expand- ing, insofar as public policy is concerned. It has been based on the political clout and access that comes with large financial contributions to political candidates and parties. The "K Street crowd"—named after the Washington boulevard on which many of corporate America's government-relations offices are located—has grown exponentially. This group can marshal com- panies and money with more impact than almost any other in- terest group can (although at times the labor unions have been almost as powerful, using the same techniques). Enron was a case study of corporate influence, having written some $6 mil- lion in checks since 1989 to almost three-quarters of all U.S. senators and half the members of the House of Representa- tives. Nevertheless, in 2001 it ranked just thirty-sixth among corporate donors.[11]

An example of how companies influenced policy is the case of the "Big Five" accounting firms throughout the 1990s. "If there was ever an example where money and lobbying damaged the public interest, this was clearly it," said former SEC chair- man Arthur Levitt in an interview with Jane Mayer of the *New Yorker*. Levitt described how the accounting firms opposed meas- ures for more accurate accounting of executive compensation for stock options. He also discussed how the firms gutted his efforts to control the potential conflicts of interest arising when accounting firms offered multiple services—such as auditing and consulting—to the same client. Their device for buying this protection? They simply conducted an end run around the SEC and showered Congress with campaign contributions. Congress, in turn, told the SEC to back off, threatening to cut its budget if Levitt didn't comply. The episode showed how those who were supposed to be the corporate watchdogs—the auditors—joined corporate America as just another member. "It was a case where the industry had more power than the regulators," Levitt said.[12] The same saga continued into 2002. As Congress moved to enact accounting reforms in June, a good deal of the business community lobbied against reform. Records showed that the accounting firms in particular had made financial contributions to 63 of the 70 members of the House Financial Services Committee and to all 21 members of the Senate Banking Committee.[13]

Another instance of how corporate clout has been marshaled in Washington for high-powered lobbying is the case of Microsoft Corporation—an important example because it is relatively new and shows how the powerful, high-tech industry embraced the K-Street culture. As late as the mid-1990s, Microsoft's Washington office consisted of just one or two people. But after the Justice Department filed its antitrust suit in 1998, the company undertook what Jeffrey Birnbaum of *Fortune* called "the largest government affairs makeover in corporate history . . . [resulting in] one of the most dominating, multifaceted and sophisticated influence machines around." The company now has a staff of fifteen in Washington; it has offices in most state capitals; it contributes heavily to right-wing think tanks like the Heritage Foundation. Microsoft is not only lobbying to defend itself against charges of being a monopoly; it is trying to influence government policies on privacy and intellectual property rights in its favor. According to *Fortune,* in the 2000 presidential election, Microsoft contributed more money to candidates than any other company did, except AT&T. Older companies have played this game for decades, but newer ones are becoming just as influential. The sum total of this corporate political clout is massive— and growing.[14]

What's more, the potential for excessive corporate influence has been highly visible. Some of it was evident when the Bush administration took office in 2001 and opened the door wide for business groups to lobby for tax cuts and the dismantling of environmental and other regulations. Bush's courting of the business community began before the inauguration, when the president-elect assembled a prominent group of business leaders at a "summit" in Austin, Texas. With virtually no substantive preparation or discussion of serious problems facing the country, the event took just a few hours. Then the CEOs emerged for the cameras, praising Bush's policies. One of the new administration's next moves was to bring in chief executives from the big energy companies to help craft the National Energy Policy, a secretive exercise that prompted the General Accounting Office to sue the administration to find out who from corporate America had participated. As time went on, the public learned not only that former energy executives held several top positions in the Bush administration—vice president, secretary of commerce, chairman of the Council on Environmental Quality, just for starters—but that companies like Enron and ExxonMobil had a strong voice on key regulatory appointments. The results showed up in tax breaks to energy companies and legislation favorable to the oil, gas, and utilities industries.[15]

Some of the strongest reflections of the deteriorating business culture came in the summer of 2002 from the Wall Street community. They came with considerable delay and no doubt with a mixture of motives that included genuine concern for the

transgressions that had taken place, fear about the negative impact that these transgressions were having on the markets, and
diversion from the role that the major financial institutions
themselves had played. "In my lifetime, American business has
never been under such scrutiny," said Henry M. Paulson Jr.,
chairman and CEO of Goldman Sachs before the National Press
Club in Washington. "To be blunt, much of it is deserved."[16] Said
Philip Purcell, chairman and CEO of Morgan Stanley Dean Witter & Co., "I think you'll see financial companies move to standards well above what's being required by regulators, legislators,
and industry organizations. If anything, the financial system has
to overcorrect."[17] It wasn't just Wall Street that was sounding
alarms. "I've been in business for forty years," said Intel's chairman Andrew Grove. "And I find myself feeling embarrassed and
ashamed by what I see in corporate America."[18]

After the September 11 attacks, corporations disingenuously
used an antiterrorist rationale to push their favorite policies, too.
Representative Edward J. Markey (D.–Mass.) described the situation this way: "No self-respecting lobbyist hasn't repackaged his
position as a patriotic response to the tragedy. The challenge is
terrorism; the answer is to re-establish telecommunications mo-
nopolies. The challenge is terrorism; the answer is to drill for oil in
the Arctic Wildlife Refuge. The challenge is terrorism; the answer
is a $15 billion retroactive tax break to scores of corporations."[19]

To be sure, today's business leaders should not be held totally
responsible for the climate in which they find themselves. The
culture of business and the standards that characterize it stem
from the society at large. The United States is a democracy; its
citizens get more or less what they ask for, or what the government and public pressure allow to happen by default. In the
1980s, when the wave of leveraged buyouts destroyed many
companies and punished their employees, American society
more than tolerated the trend. The mass media turned corporate

raiders into rock stars, and Washington, along with almost everyone else, applauded. In the 1990s, America cheered as the Dow
Jones and breathless CNBC newscasters became the barome-
ters of the national health and welfare. Large institutional investors—who used highly sophisticated computer programs to
churn their stock holdings with the quarterly performance of
companies—have played a big role in the short-term horizons
of capital markets, putting excruciating pressure on CEOs to do
whatever they could to pump up their share prices at the expense
of the longer-term value of their companies. True, some Americans, like the famed investor Warren Buffett, warned against over-
investing in companies that showed little or no earnings, but there
were very few of them. When Alan Greenspan protested that the
markets were in the grip of an irrational exuberance, he could
have been talking about American society in its broadest sense.

But CEOs are now in the crosshairs. Unless they attempt to
dig themselves out of the reputational black hole that they are
in, they cannot be major players on the national and international stage in the way they should be. Their redemption will not
be easy. "On the road to deregulation, the basic building blocks
of capitalism—clarity, transparency, fairness, openness—were
sacrificed," wrote Bruce Nussbaum of *Business Week* in the wake
of the Enron collapse. "Everything the public needs to evaluate
risk, value stocks, and participate in the equity culture was undermined."[20] From shoring up the credibility of financial reporting to scrupulous adherence to the new campaign financing laws,
CEOs need to be out front in pushing and executing reforms—
or government will do it for them.

One crucial imperative is for business leaders to embrace campaign finance reform. In March 2002, Congress finally passed,
and President Bush signed, legislation mandating the first major

changes since the Watergate era in the way political contributions are made. Among other things, the new law limits so-called soft-money donations to political parties by corporations, unions, and wealthy individuals that are designed to influence federal elections. It also limits the way political advertising can be financed. These rules will encourage a less incestuous interaction between companies and politicians, but the enactment of this legislation does not mean the problem is solved. The new law is already being challenged in the courts; it could be modified or even declared unconstitutional. There is also the possibility that they will be interpreted by the highly politicized Federal Election Commission in such a way as to weaken the intent of the law. In addition, there are other ways that corporations can raise large amounts of funds and direct them to parties and candidates. For example, although the legislation caps soft money, CEOs and other top executives may well attempt to retain their grip on politicians by becoming more active in soliciting hard money, in smaller amounts, from employees and friends. They can still buy influence by giving large sums to political parties at the state level, particularly to states that are pivotal in national elections. "Backers and opponents [of the new law] are vehemently at odds over whether the bill will lift the moral tone of American electoral competition or increase corruption and trample the First Amendment," wrote John Harwood and David Rogers in the *Wall Street Journal*. "But both sides agree on two points: The prospective law won't take money out of politics."[21]

Some observers are certain that business leaders will exploit every loophole in the law. But there is another possibility. CEOs could take the offensive to push reform even further. They could lobby for the establishment of a government agency that will be a vigilant and tough monitor of campaign finance activities. The Federal Elections Commission, which is supposed to play that role now, is widely acknowledged to be ineffective and ought to be replaced with a more independent agency that has the stature of the SEC and the ability to enforce the law. In addition, a number of top executives could just say "no." They could band together as a group and decide to stay out of campaign finance politics altogether. In so doing, they would suffer no competitive disadvantages with one another. They would be declaring the end of political shakedowns. Do they have the courage to do this? They might, if they fully understood the importance of restoring their tattered reputation.

The stakes for business leaders in improving their standing in society are huge. At some level, most CEOs no doubt understand them. But the pressure of their day-to-day tasks—to meet stock market expectations; to service customers; to develop, empower, and inspire employees—may well have blinded many chief executives to the precarious position of big business in America today. For example, CEOs may not think hard enough about the rise of a perpetual national-security state and the gradual but inexorable expansion of government regulation. If so, they underestimate the strength of forces working to reverse the trend toward increasingly open markets. They may decide that the fallout from Enron and Arthur Andersen will eventually pass with minimal impact, especially as the economy recovers and the stock market rises. Yet in a nation in which so many citizens have their future tied up with Wall Street, the backlash against perceived corporate abuses may only be starting. Business leaders may feel particularly emboldened by what they see as the superiority of American management and technology, believing that they are poised to lead the global economy no matter what the political environment might be. But this sense that the momentum for American-led globalization is unstoppable may turn out to be appallingly naive.

To play a more influential role in national and international policy, CEOs must do more than repair their collective reputation.

They will also have to see their responsibilities extending beyond insuring the health of their own companies or industries. They are not organized for this now. The voice of the business community is fragmented by countless business organizations that lobby on behalf of their members and no one else. Most of the groups are transparently self-serving and frequently headed by men and women—often former officials from the U.S. executive branch or Congress—who are knowledgeable about Washington but not about the real business world itself. These group heads are adept at shepherding their corporate bosses inside the beltway, introducing them to this cabinet officer and that senator. What gets lost in this pattern of action is the initiative of the CEOs themselves, who have become captives of the system. If interaction with Washington is considered only as something to be delegated, chief executives will give the big public issues—those not specific to their companies—as little time as possible. We will be getting not the best of corporate America, but the thoughts of a shadow government bureaucracy in Washington that is thinking and acting for America's top business executives.

Business leaders will have to devote time to considering where the United States and the rest of the world should be headed and how they can contribute to the realization of that vision. This kind of disinterested thinking will not come easy to them. CEOs are understandably obsessed with competitive pressures and Wall Street's demands for quarterly profits. On any given day, they are likely to spend at least twelve hours on some combination of strategic and budget reviews, media interviews about the latest financial results, hiring and firing top-level staff, making merger or divestiture decisions, and traveling. Carving out time to think about public policy is enormously difficult.

A more constructive and informed government-business partnership also assumes that many Americans are willing to leave behind some of their ideological baggage. In the United States, the relations between the public and private sectors have for generations often been characterized by mutual ignorance of each other's world, suspicion of each other's intentions, and even hostility toward each other's goals. The nation needs a change in this highly politicized environment. It is not productive to hold out the vision of truly free markets when clearly all the modern economies are mixed economies, with so many critical sectors— finance, transportation, communication, energy, health care—all subject to substantial regulation. We should abandon such loaded expressions as "industrial policy" and "corporate welfare" and move toward a vision of market-oriented policies supported by thoughtful and effective regulation. In this way—at the top levels, at least—government and business would be pursuing together a number of critical objectives: long-term policies for economic growth, a fairer distribution of that growth at home and abroad, a cleaner and healthier environment in America and overseas. Unless business and government leaders can get beyond these ideological fetishes, CEOs will not be trusted to play a larger role on the national and international stage.

In the summer of 2002, there were some indications that the business community was waking up to the challenge that faced them. The New York Stock Exchange issued a report elevating corporate governance standards for the companies that listed on the Big Board. It followed a much weaker report by the Business Roundtable. Standard & Poor's, the credit-rating agency, announced tougher rules for its evaluation of companies' accounts. The Conference Board announced the establishment of a Commission on Public Trust and Private Enterprise, chaired by Peter G. Peterson, chairman of The Blackstone Group, and John Snow, chairman and CEO of CSX Corporation, to examine the broader questions of restoring integrity to the markets and to corporate

America. As noted, a few top business executives began to speak out. But important as they are, these efforts were nowhere near enough to deal with the magnitude of the problem.

As a precondition for real business leadership, a number of CEOs, current and past, and key government officials, must want to lead the way. America has no shortage of highly capable candidates in the business establishment. For all the criticism of big business today, the talent pool is indeed impressive. Besides active CEOs, an even richer vein may be the numerous recently retired executives. In today's world, in which retirement comes early and life spans are longer, many former business leaders have decades of public service in front of them, if they choose this course. These men and women will have an easier time being objective and being seen as such. They need nothing from Washington. They don't have to worry about how their views will reflect on their companies, because the government and the public would understand that they are no longer part of them.

Among the active top business leaders, few stand out as Robert Rubin, chairman of the executive committee of Citigroup and formerly chairman of Goldman Sachs, as well as Secretary of the Treasury. Almost no one else has his range of experience and widespread respect. Peter Peterson, chairman of The Blackstone Group and former U.S. secretary of commerce, has been a national leader on fiscal policy, global trade, and foreign relations. Philip Condit, chairman and CEO of The Boeing Company, is a leader in the aerospace and defense industries. His CEO, Richard Parsons, is also one of the nation's top executives. Andrew Grove of Intel understands advanced computer technology as few do. Carly Fiorina, chairman and CEO of Hewlett-Packard, and Patricia Russo, CEO of Lucent Technologies, are both national leaders in technology, too. Henry Paulson Jr., chairman and CEO of Goldman Sachs, has extensive experience in the world of global finance. Michael Dell, chairman and CEO of Dell Computer Corporation, is at the forefront of the global revolution in manufacturing. Kenneth Chennault, chairman and CEO of American Express Company, has a superb understanding of cultures around the world. Dr. John Rowe Jr., chairman and CEO of Aetna Inc., is a national leader in health care. Shelly Lazarus, chairman and CEO of Ogilvy & Mather Worldwide, brings deep knowledge of public relations. William Clay Ford Jr., chairman and CEO of Ford, aspires to be a world leader in the environmental movement. Jeffrey Immelt, chairman and CEO of GE, has a keen understanding of many industries and countries, as does Samuel Palmisano, CEO of IBM. Fred Smith, chairman and CEO of Federal Express Corporation, has revolutionized the global transportation system. C. Michael Armstrong, chairman and CEO of AT&T, has exceptional experience in the computer, defense, and telecommunications industries. Richard Grasso, chairman and CEO of the New York Stock Exchange, has not only managed the Big Board in exemplary fashion, but also played a pivotal role in America's rebound from September 11, and in pushing for more effective corporate governance after Enron. Many more chief executives belong on this list.

The list of notable former CEOs is equally impressive. Louis V. Gerstner Jr. managed a spectacular turnaround at IBM and is passionate about education. Jack Welch brings an understanding of management that few can equal. Gerald Levin, former chief executive of AOL Time Warner, knows the global media and entertainment industry from every angle. Roger Enrico, who ran PepsiCo; Ralph Larsen, who ran Johnson & Johnson; John Pepper, who oversaw Procter & Gamble; Lawrence Bossidy, who headed up Honeywell International; Harvey Golub, who revived American Express; William George, who chaired Medtronic; Henry Schacht, who ran Cummings Engine Company and Lucent; Gerald Greenwald, who ran United Airlines; and J. Michael Cook, who oversaw Deloitte Touche Tohmatsu—

all are examples of the best of corporate America and have substantial potential for public service.

Up and coming is a generation of business leaders who also ought to involve themselves at least enough to grow into a bigger role in the future. Robert B. Willumstad is a potential heir apparent at Citigroup; Stanley O'Neal will soon be chairman and CEO of Merrill Lynch; Paul Otellini, president and chief operating officer of Intel, is likely to be its next leader; Indra Nooyi, president of PepsiCo, is second in command there; William Weldon will be the next chief of Johnson & Johnson; Heidi Miller, CFO of BankOne Corporation, is one of the nation's corporate stars.

In identifying a business leadership cohort, an effective organization must include far more diversity than existed in the Committee for Economic Development (CED) or its counterparts in the 1940s, when there were no female chief executives and virtually none from minority ethnic groups. Chief executives who oversee firms that may have headquarters abroad but substantial operations in the United States need to be part of the effort, too. Thus Lord John Browne, CEO of British Petroleum plc; Jorma Ollila, chairman and CEO of Nokia Corporation; Heinrich V. Pierer, CEO of Siemens AG; Nobuyuki Idei, chairman and CEO of Sony Corporation; and others like them should be involved.

At the same time, business leaders will need to persuade the Bush administration to foster a higher level of CEO involvement in policy making along the lines of the original CED or Economic Cooperation Administration (ECA). Bush and his cabinet may well not want to endorse a new vision for business leadership, or fully understand what is at stake. Perhaps they will not wish to share their power. In the 1940s, Commerce Secretary Jesse Jones was a strong supporter of powerful business associations that could influence public policy, because he needed America's corporations on his side to spur and direct the postwar economic revival—to get production going, to create jobs.

He understood that in a modern industrial economy, the inter-play of public and private power was crucial. Moreover, Jones was supported by a president who, though highly suspicious of the motives of big business, knew that he had to work closely with it.

How to read the Bush administration? It came into office with unusual CEO credentials (Bush himself, Dick Cheney, Paul O'Neill, Donald Rumsfeld, Donald Evans, among others) and touting its desire to be friendly to business. From the start, the administration seemed to give business executives free rein to formulate administration policy. Then, after the Enron mess, the administration moved quickly to distance itself from direct and visible business influence. Clearly, neither of these extremes is a basis for the kind of business-government relationship now re-quired. It's not about clubhouse buddies, not about informal kitchen cabinets, not about rallying CEOs to support this or that piece of urgent legislation. The big question is whether the Bush administration can summon a view of what it *is* about.

As summer 2002 arrived, there was evidence that President Bush and his team understood the gravity of events and were mov-ing more aggressively to address them. There was more talk about the importance of government-business cooperation on homeland security. On the question of corporate behavior in financial mar-kets, Secretary of Treasury Paul O'Neill, formerly chairman and CEO of Alcoa, Inc., minced few words. "I think anyone who is paying attention ought to be outraged about the [corporate revela-tions] that keep tumbling out," he told ABC's *This Week*.[22] Said SEC chairman Harvey Pitt, who once was a defender of corpora-tions accused of malfeasance, at Stanford Law School, "It would be hard to overstate the need to remedy the loss of confidence."[23]

There are many reasons why President Bush should take an interest in building a new kind of government-business coali-tion. From the day he took power, many have perceived his ties with business as a bad caricature of Republican coziness with

CEOs. Consequently, the administration might enjoy substantial benefits in recasting that relationship. Then, too, the government needs a lot of help. It is overwhelmed by the demands of homeland security; it is not sure how to react to Enron and its wider implications; it has lost its grip on fiscal policy and is at sea when it comes to the future of health care and Social Security; it is facing serious problems in its international economic and foreign policy.

Let me explain what I'm *not* advocating. I don't want to see a new military-industrial complex, in which the relationship of government and business is too intertwined—that is, in which the government is the nation's largest contractor and customer and manipulates business with the lure of subsidies, tax breaks, and the relaxation of antitrust policy. Even in an era of more government-business cooperation, the relationship needs a healthy tension between the two, and vigilance on the part of both so that the partnership strengthens rather than subverts free enterprise. This balance will not be easy when national security is the paramount concern and when government involvement in the economy is growing. Although business should not be in outright opposition to the government, neither should it be totally compliant.

I'm not suggesting that there be one omnibus business organization that purports to speak for the entire private sector and that supplants the trade associations that do exist. This would be politically impossible and highly undesirable, given the range and complexity of the important challenges requiring attention. Nor should businesses stop lobbying for their firms or industries. This activity is, after all, at the intersection of democracy and capitalism. Moreover, individual CEOs are going to have personal and professional relationships with top government officials. As long as campaign finance reforms are effectively implemented, these relationships will also be an important and constructive part of a new business-government alliance.

Individual CEOs also demonstrate considerable civic-mindedness, including generosity toward philanthropic causes. Many serve on government-sponsored task forces and spend time offering personal advice to public officials. In the environmental realm, many executives are leading their companies toward responsible policies for environmental protection. A number of CEOs share their views in speeches, interviews, op-ed articles, and books. In advocating a wider role for business leaders and a deeper partnership with government, I am not suggesting any slowdown of these worthy efforts. Rather, we need to look beyond the role of CEOs acting just as individuals; both the business community and the nation require a more collective effort.

If the business leaders can meet the challenges I have described, they will have much to offer the country. With their knowledge of markets and technology, they have a finely honed habit of delivering results. They can inject a much-needed element of market reality into the government's economic policies. They can be especially important in helping to shape economic policy at home and abroad. Enmeshed in worldwide commercial and financial networks and experienced in managing culturally diverse workforces, business leaders interact on a daily basis with dozens of governments and international institutions; they are in a position to know better than most the importance of integrating public and private interests in an international setting. On a global scale, business leaders can help lead the way toward collaboration across borders and a reduction of political, cultural, and ethnic tensions.

The involvement of CEOs with governments is crucial for another reason. Markets have become far bigger, far more powerful, and far more complex in the last few decades. They are no longer segmented into separate compartments that can be easily analyzed and supervised. For example, banking, securities, insurance, energy, and commodity trading are all interdependent, and the same can be said for telecommunications, the media, and the entertainment industries. No government can oversee today's markets with old regulatory models. A new model is essential—one in which corporate self-regulation is intensified, but in which the government has access to timely information and is in a position to monitor activity and mete out effective disciplinary measures. Exactly how this model should be designed and implemented are issues that government and business must work out together in the context of different clusters of industries. But a partnership between government and business leaders who are acting in the public interest can lower the odds that regulations are too lax or too stringent.

The United States plays a unique role in the world because of its unrivaled military and economic power. It is a major leadership role, encompassing not just government and the military but also the business community. Companies abroad are increasingly adopting American business techniques: American systems of accounting and corporate governance (Enron and Andersen notwithstanding), American technology and management, and American business education. This puts a special responsibility on U.S. chief executives to show that they care about the nation's political, legal, economic, and social foundations and are ready to make them stronger.

CHAPTER 4

PROTECTING THE HOMELAND

W HEN TERRORISTS STRUCK the World Trade Center and the Pentagon, Washington responded as quickly as it could. It closed down all civilian air traffic. It moved to seal the Mexican and Canadian borders. Top government officials were escorted to safe locations. Meanwhile, the stock exchanges were shuttered, leading to the suspension of the rhythm of global capitalism itself. When the New York Stock Exchange opened its door six days later, stock prices plunged and many in government and the investment community wondered whether a financial crash was imminent.

It is difficult to capture the fears and emotions of September 11 and its immediate aftermath. The images of planes flying into the World Trade Center, of people running from the collapsing buildings, of Mayor Rudolph Giuliani and other officials calming the nation—they will remain with us for a lifetime. On one level people were frightened of the unknown. On another, many Americans realized that the open society they had taken for granted—open borders, open markets, freedom to move around—was at best threatened and at worst taken from them forever. On September 12, Americans had no clear vision of their collective future. Would there be a second wave of attacks? Would the next one be aimed at our nuclear energy plants, our water systems, our bridges and tunnels? There seemed little doubt that the responsibility for the people's protection lay with government—but below the level of the president, who would be responsible for what? How would state, local, and city officials enter into the picture? What would happen to the economy? Would national security requirements eclipse civil liberties, and would the United States evolve into a police state? Hendrik Hertzberg of the *New Yorker,* writing in the immediate aftermath of the attacks, put it this way: "The catastrophe . . . turned the foot of Manhattan into the mouth of hell. . . . The events were seen as through a glass, brightly. It took hours to begin to comprehend their magnitude; it is taking days for the defensive numbness they induced to wear off; it will take months—or years—to measure their impact and meaning."[1]

In the several months after the attacks, the United States began the job of getting organized for what would be known as "homeland security." It was a monumental challenge. Eight months after September 11, for example, there were large gaps in the protection of virtually everything, from air travel, to the security of nuclear reactors, to the public health system. Because the United States has national grids for electricity, communication, and transportation, all connected to one another, the vulnerability of the nation's critical infrastructure remained a big concern. The United States needed time just to determine where the major problems were. And it needed even more time to reorganize the government to deal with them.

Another factor came into play: the realization that most of America's critical infrastructure was in the hands of the private sector. The challenge then became—and remains—how business and government could best cooperate to protect the infrastructure. But protection alone isn't enough. The nation has to guard against terrorism without destroying the very fabric of its society: It must keep the cost of doing business low and preserve the vibrancy of U.S. markets and Americans' capacity to innovate, while keeping its borders open and preserving the civil liberties on which American society rests. The nation may not be able to do all that its citizens would like, but business leaders should help make the best possible trade-offs. "Government needs to partner with the private sector to share resources and expertise," said Tom Ridge, U.S. director of homeland security, at a conference in the spring of 2002. "Our goals are the same: increase security, improve preparedness. It's more important than ever before that we find ways to work together."[2]

The attacks of September 11 changed the environment for American business as few events could have. Recessions cause major disruptions, but they occur with reasonable regularity. New technologies, such as the steam engine, the telephone, the internal combustion engine, the Internet, are rarer occurrences, but business has a long history of dealing with them. Companies have accommodated many wars in the last century: World War II, Korea, Vietnam, the Gulf War. What makes terrorism so different and difficult is that it affects everything—the economy, everyday safety, foreign policy. It undermines people's confidence and infects their sense of well-being. And it will be a long time before it's over, if it ever is. As Vice President Dick Cheney told the Council on Foreign Relations in the winter of 2002, "The war against terror will not end in a treaty. There will be no summit meeting, no negotiations with terrorists. The conflict can only end in their complete and utter destruction."[3]

What are the implications of this open-ended, insidious, and violent conflict for business leaders? No one can gauge what the impact of another attack in the near future would be—whether it would simply accelerate efforts already under way to protect the country or cause a draconian response going beyond anything now contemplated. But this much we do know: A new set of important problems must now compete for CEOs' attention. As detailed in chapter 1, no matter what happens, for example, doing business will become more costly, as the expense of everything from travel, to insurance, to the protection of data will escalate.

The cost of insurance deserves particular emphasis, because there could be significant discontinuities. Many analysts believe the cost of property and business-disruption insurance could increase by 200 percent in urban centers. Sanford C. Bernstein & Co., a Wall Street brokerage firm, estimates that rising insurance costs could reduce profits in 2002 by 1.5 to 2 percent on average and by 5 to 10 percent in sectors like transportation.[4]

Operations will become more complex, because businesses must pay more attention to their people, their facilities, and their links to suppliers, customers, and partners. Leadership qualities will be tested as employees feel insecure and look to CEOs for reassurance.

Political risks abroad will escalate as American foreign policy becomes more aggressive and militant (as further discussed in chapter 10). CEOs will have to give more careful attention to existing operations overseas, not to mention whether to expand their foreign investments.

Business leaders will also find themselves more enmeshed with the government. The mixed U.S. economy, characterized by an intricate web of business and government relationships, will become even more interconnected. We can expect more government regulation for cyberspace, transportation, money transfers, immigration and border control, public health, and so forth. We can envision government-imposed standards for private security guards, for investigating the background of employees, and for the protection of corporate information-technology facilities. To assure a more accurate picture of the condition of a company, the Securities and Exchange Commission could possibly require security audits appended to financial accounts. The extent of new regulation will depend on two things: whether there are additional terrorist attacks, and whether business leaders are themselves giving homeland security a high enough priority to preempt the need for government intervention.

Today homeland security is the nation's number one priority. We now know that even the most extreme scenarios, once seemingly remote, are possible. But it is also clear that protecting the United States completely will never be possible, the best efforts notwithstanding. In a widely cited article in *How Did This Happen?*, an anthology on terrorism, Coast Guard Commander Stephen Flynn paints a picture of the massive amount of traffic that passed through American border inspection systems in 2000: 489 million people, 127 million passenger vehicles, 11.6 million maritime containers, 11.5 million trucks, 2.2 million rail cars, 829,000 planes, and 211,000 vessels. Meeting the organizational challenges of dealing with such a porous nation will take many years, if it can be done at all.[5]

From the standpoint of business leaders, several requirements are immediate. Foremost is the need to put in place mechanisms to protect their employees in the event of catastrophe. Then comes the task of establishing procedures to insure business continuity through the protection of everything from facilities to data storage. A third job is securing networks—such as taking care of information systems and supplier relationships. A fourth priority is the implementation of ongoing systems to keep people in the company alert to terrorism threats, to train them for emergencies, and ultimately to embed such knowledge and behavior into a firm's DNA. These measures compel a new way of thinking about business strategy and organization, including considerations of where to locate a business, where to establish redundant capabilities, and how to redesign supply chains. They require an added element of leadership: the ability not just to manage in a volatile world economy but to lead during extreme threats to life itself. Suffice it to say, none of this is taught in universities, and very few business leaders have had the requisite on-the-job training.

Although the government cannot deliver on its promise of security without the cooperation of the private sector, the reverse is also true. "Underlying [an] enterprise-based examination of the firm's needs and prospects is . . . the requirement for . . . a reengagement with government at all levels," wrote Ralph W. Shrader, chairman and CEO of Booz • Allen & Hamilton, Inc., and Mike McConnell, former director of the National Security Agency, in *Strategy + Business*.[6] The point seems uncontroversial. The United States spends roughly $110 billion a year on security (including federal, state, and local police, but not armed forces). Of this, business expenditures account for about $55 billion. Indeed, a broad business-government partnership, encompassing many different projects around the nation, is emerging, although it is far from being well coordinated or having a coherent strategy. Business has been working with government to install tracking technology in airports, at seaports, and at border crossings. Together they are also creating systems to track the flows of money and more effectively share data between government agencies. The public and private sectors are collaborating on policy guidelines for cyber-security, food inspection, and bioterrorism. A host of other shared endeavors is possible for the development, building, and distribution of products and services. These include sophisticated software that allows agencies to track, analyze, and coordinate massive amounts of real-time data; equipment that uses biometrics to recognize selected individuals in crowds; and biological and chemical detection equipment. In remarks before the Electronics Industries Association in late April 2002, Tom Ridge envisioned what some companies of the future might do:

> If I were writing that story I might include . . . biometric systems that help keep the Winter Olympics terror free and can do the same for airports and subway systems; next generation detection, which can sniff out chemical and biological weapons from the air; dashboard electronics that can help trucks and their cargo reduce the border crossing from two or three hours to matters of seconds; simulation software that enables cities to test their responses to any attack scenario one can imagine.[7]

But all this is just a start. Government and business, with universities and other nonprofit institutions, need to create early-warning systems, so that the country can respond much more quickly to attacks than it could previously. The nation will require communications systems that will enable federal, state, and local agencies—and companies—to immediately link up in an emergency. Such systems, for example, will alert public health officials when there is an unusual increase in disease outbreaks and would trigger an immediate investigation into whether bioterrorism might be involved in a particular event or group of events. In all these areas, private enterprise will be deeply involved, providing technology, helping with logistics, and participating in management.

An example of the kind of emerging business-government cooperation is a "war game" conducted over two days in December 2001 under the auspices of the global consulting firm of Booz • Allen & Hamilton. For two days, a group of CEOs and other senior business executives, with officials of the Departments of Defense and Health and Human Resources, the Federal Emergency Management Agency, and state and local governments, worked out how they would respond to a terrorist attack involving the release of aerosolized pneumonic plague bacteria in two major cities. The symptoms of the plague resemble the flu, but the disease is nearly 100 percent fatal. The war-game participants realized how quickly the systems for public health care, law enforcement, and social services could be overwhelmed. They saw how inefficiently local, state, and federal government agencies worked together—and how inefficiently business would work with these agencies. Among the participants' recommendations were the establishment of single points of contact at every facility and agency and prearranged, in-place mechanisms to collect and share information and disseminate decisions. The participants reported that the difference between a controlled outbreak and a massive epidemic depends on coordinated leadership, on knowing who is in charge at every level, on reliable information about stockpiles and distribution systems around the nation, and on exquisite coordination between sectors: "Preparedness will require new levels of communication and cooperation across public/private, local/national, and military/civilian boundaries."[8]

Another example of the kind of cooperation that is emerging is the Business Roundtable (BRT) homeland security task force, led by C. Michael Armstrong, chairman and CEO of AT&T. One focus of the group has been to establish a secure communications network that will connect the 150 CEOs who make up the BRT, wherever they are in the world, within minutes, in the event of an emergency. The purpose is to share information and coordinate responses to a crisis. The network will allow these top corporate executives to interact with senior government officials under tight security and authentication procedures, around the clock. Armstrong envisions that a subsequent stage of the project would allow BRT executives to connect with nonmember CEOs. For example, various BRT leaders would be able to connect with others in their respective industries.[9]

Other kinds of cooperation involve partnerships between business and nongovernmental organizations. In February 2002, at the World Economic Forum in New York, a new, independent not-for-profit organization called the Disaster Response Network (DRN) was established. Comprising prominent engineering and transportation companies—including Parsons Brinckeroff, Bechtel Group, Inc., and Leo A. Daly—the network will respond to calls for help in an emergency, sending rescue equipment with other specialized services in the event of a disaster. The group intends not just to supply people and equipment but to expedite the response using management capabilities and information systems in the business world. The DRN is focused on mobilizing the business community during the phase that immediately follows a disaster but before reconstruction begins. Its mission is to respond to the calls of official relief agencies such as the Red Cross. As a Web-based clearinghouse for information and a human network for business leaders, the DRN will also design training programs for businesses and contract for advice on legal matters pertaining to liability. In 2002, the network is concentrating on recruiting companies in the engineering, construction, logistics, and transportation sectors, but in 2003 it is extending membership to other industries. From its inception, too, the DRN has seen itself as an international organization; already by 2002, its participants included companies from England, Spain, Switzerland, Greece, Mexico, and India.[10]

There are other examples of the potential for more government-business cooperation. Localities and states are forming their own terrorist task forces. Los Angeles County, for example, has established the Terrorism Early Warning Group, which is concerned with the security of the local airports, harbors, bridges, and theme parks. The purpose of the team—which includes police, firefighters, hospital administrators, and local business leaders—is to plan emergency responses through the advance knowledge of how the responsibilities will be apportioned, for example, which hospitals will be immediately available and what transportation can be used. Massachusetts has created the Statewide Anti-Terrorism Unified Response Network, asking each municipality in the state to organize itself along the lines of what Los Angeles County has done.

These kinds of efforts are mirrored by the activities of some industry associations. The Pharmaceutical Research and Manufacturing Association, for example, has launched an outreach program to educate both business and government officials about bioterrorism issues and solutions. Academic institutions are also acting in collaborative ways with business and government. Dartmouth's Institute for Security Technology is bringing together groups from around the nation to create a national research and development agenda for cyber-security. Colorado State University is doing the same, but in the area of biological safety, with its new Rocky Mountain Institute for Biosecurity Research. In sum, various organizations are initiating substantial activity. Because this activity encompasses the private sector, the opportunity for business leadership is substantial.

For the future, business leaders can undertake several measures to contribute significantly to homeland security in general and the protection of critical infrastructure in particular.

AGENDA ITEM: THE ADMINISTRATION
AND BUSINESS LEADERS SHOULD
INSURE THAT THE HOMELAND
SECURITY ADVISORY COUNCIL
IS ACCORDED THE SCOPE AND
IMPORTANCE IT DESERVES

Because there is so much going on in the homeland security arena, so much money being thrown at the problem, and so many collaborative public-private endeavors—and because all this is in such an early stage—the single most important task for CEOs and their government counterparts is to establish an effective oversight mechanism. Tom Ridge proposed a Homeland Security Advisory Council on March 19, 2002. According to the charter, the council would contain twenty-one members, drawn from private industry, academia, nongovernmental organizations, and state and local governments. The council would oversee several senior advisory committees, including one made up of business leaders. On June 5, 2002, President Bush proposed the establishment of a cabinet-level Department for Homeland Security, combining twenty-two federal agencies comprised of 170,000 employees, with an initial budget of $38 billion. Shortly afterwards, he appointed sixteen members of the advisory council originally proposed by Ridge. The group's chairman is Joseph J. Grano, chairman and CEO of UBS Paine Webber. Other business leaders include Sidney Taurel, chairman and CEO of Eli Lilly and Co.; Lydia Waters Thomas, president and CEO of Mitretek Systems, Inc.; Paul Bremer III, chairman and CEO of Marsh Crisis Consulting; and Kathleen M. Bader, Business Group President of Dow Chemical Co.[11] Here are some of the issues that the council should address:

What precisely are the priorities, and in what
order should they be addressed?

There is a real risk that in an attempt to protect everyone and everything right away, the organizations involved may undermine the entire effort by trying to do too much at once. Because many U.S. communications, transportation, and supply systems are linked, any security effort must secure these nodes above all. There are other "choke points" that need to be addressed first.

Indeed, for all the efforts of Washington, corporate America, and other groups, by mid-2002 the overall homeland security strategy was still unclear. A study by the Brookings Institution suggested that the effort was too preoccupied with preventing the specific kinds of attacks that had taken place already—such as airline hijacking or anthrax transmission through the mail— rather than on more generalized protection. The Brookings study recommends a much stronger perimeter defense at the borders, a more intense focus on potential terrorists within the United States, a prioritization of where the nation is most vulnerable (that is, where hundreds or thousands of Americans could be killed). The study singles out for priority attention seaport containers coming into the United States with hazardous material, because only 2 to 3 percent of incoming cargo is now inspected. Brookings also points to hazardous material that is routinely trucked around the country, and to the possibility of someone's introducing a high-quality biological agent into the ventilation of large buildings. The study's main point—and it is the right one—is the need for a more strategic policy in place of the seemingly scatter-shot approach now employed.[12]

Is public and private money being spent wisely?

It's hard to know whether the funding for homeland security is too much or too little without an agreed-upon framework. Congresswoman Jane Harman (D.–Calif.) put it this way: "The administration gave us a budget before it gave us a strategy. . . . [U]ntil we have a strategy there is no sensible way to put our resources, which are not infinite, against our biggest vulnerabilities."[13] The president's proposed budget for 2002–2003 has earmarked $38 billion for homeland security, a threefold increase from previous budgets. Many of these programs will be new and could easily become pork-barrel projects for influential senators and congressional representatives, not to mention the administration itself. CEOs and government officials need to establish an auditing process that will inform Congress and the public about the full panoply of programs. Business leaders should also help one another and the government assess the totality of private spending on homeland security, asking these questions: What does the full public-private picture look like? Does it reflect the most important national goals?

What should be the regulatory model for overseeing business's compliance with security mandates from the government?

Over the next several years, every level of government will be asking the private sector to institute certain measures in the national antiterrorism campaign. There are at least two major challenges for formulating public policy that supports rather than subverts markets. First, government and business ought to determine how to avoid multiple regulatory directives that are neither coordinated nor evaluated for adverse collateral economic impact. Second, government and business leaders should determine now—before the patterns are set—where industry self-regulation can be established.

Do business and government have an effective framework for measuring the costs and benefits of new regulations relating to homeland security?

Often the problem is not the absence of a law or regulation but weak adherence to, and enforcement of, what is already on the books. Just as often, new government mandates require more information from companies—while federal agencies cannot even process the material they already have. Another big problem is the inevitable regulatory creep. As new laws come into effect quickly, as is happening, they are often filled with holes and need extensive clarification and interpretation. The resulting mandates become voluminous and constitute serious impediments to business efficiency. Because homeland security could become so all-encompassing from a regulatory standpoint, the measures need some mechanism at the outset to balance the true benefits to security against the regulatory costs. These costs include the time it takes to achieve compliance, the effectiveness of new rules, and the impediments that the rules could impose on the smooth functioning of markets. There is a strong case, for example, for a homeland-security regulatory-impact statement, which could work as follows: Given the special urgency of national security concerns, an agency could quickly impose new regulations. The regulations, however, would automatically be repealed in, say, two years unless a special judicial panel, established by the government and including business and other leaders, determined that, all things considered, the importance of the regulation outweighed its costs.

Are the proper laws in place to protect corporate liability?

The private sector is being asked to share proprietary information with the government, some of which could ultimately disclose a company's lack of preparedness. Inevitably, this information will become public. Aside from jeopardizing the security of valuable commercial data, CEOs could be opening themselves up to lawsuits if they divulge flaws in their security systems. The advisory council should be asking what kind of laws legislators must pass to deal with this possibility, for unless business is protected, the necessary cooperation may not materialize. A similar issue exists regarding antitrust liability. As industries cooperate with one another on security policies, they will need to gain some exemption from accusations of collusion in restraint of trade.

Is the homeland security effort being adequately assessed against other critical criteria, such as the preservation of essential privacy?

Business is developing a range of new technologies that will allow the gathering and centralization of data from a wide range of sources. For example, the Association of Motor Vehicle Administrators is seeking federal money to create a single standard for drivers' licenses that will link all fifty state motor vehicle databases into a single, integrated system. It would be a short distance from that to national identity cards, which would contain a wealth of information gleaned from individuals' credit history, health records, and encounters—small and large—with the criminal justice system. In a not-so-far-fetched scenario, these cards could be used for everyday purposes such as entering buildings, bringing highly personal information to a wide range of people, such as security guards. Such possibilities, which represent the intersection of the Internet age and terrorism, raise profound questions for all groups in contemporary society—including business leaders, who, after all, will be at the forefront of new technological developments. Jeffrey Rosen, of George Washington University Law School, captured the issue in the *New York Times Magazine* in April 2002: "When the e-business technologies of tracking, classifying, profiling and monitoring were used to identify the preferences of American consumers . . . Silicon Valley could argue that it was serving the cause of freedom and individual choice," he wrote. "But when the same software applications are used by the government to track, classify, profile and monitor American citizens, they become not technologies of liberty but technologies of state surveillance."[14] Business leaders should play a role in the judgment of where to draw the lines, a judgment that they should make not just on the basis of commercial self-interest. Privacy is just one aspect of the larger question of civil liberties, of course. The detention of thousands of people on secret charges, the monitoring of conversations between lawyers and clients, the plan to establish military tribunals, the expansion of criminal profiling, the shift in the modus vivendi of law enforcement from investigating completed crimes to preventing future ones—all this is part of homeland security. Americans need to monitor these measures to make sure that the best possible balance remains between antiterrorism activities and personal freedom.

Under what circumstances should the U.S. government intervene to protect or otherwise shore up U.S. industries?

In the wake of September 11, Washington rushed to create a financial package for the airline industry. As late as June 2002, it was still wrestling with how to support the insurance industry. In retrospect, these were highly chaotic efforts in response to what was perceived as an overwhelming emergency. Given that senior government executives from President Bush on down predict that more terrorism is certain, now is the time to fashion guidelines for government subsidies to business. When are they justified? What should be the quid pro quo from business?

How should the new department of homeland security be structured to deal with the private sector?

When President Bush announced the new department, public attention was focused on which agencies were in and which were not—particularly the intelligence-gathering agencies. There was almost no attention to the links between the department and business. The advisory council should focus on this critical relationship. The creation of a new department affords a special opportunity to build a modern infrastructure for a public-private partnership, one characterized less by the hierarchies and bureaucratic rigidities that are found in traditional government agencies than by the latest communications technologies and flatter and more flexible organizational structures. Given the enormous public-private agenda, these structural problems are critical to solve early on. Writing in May 2002, David J. Rothkopf, CEO of Intellibridge, Inc., painted the worrisome lack of adequate preparation. "To date, companies have been involved in very little of the coordinated planning, drilling exercises, threat evaluation, intelligence sharing, cooperative research, or any other steps a [homeland security] strategy requires."[15] There's no time to waste.

How can government and business avoid creating the equivalent of a security-industrial complex, outside the normal boundaries of free markets?

In the Cold War, a military-industrial complex was built up, with exceptionally deep relationships between defense contractors and the Pentagon. The new advisory council ought to examine what the lessons are for the nation today—both positive and negative. This is not a theoretical question. Existing industries, many in the computer and software arena, see major business opportunities in selling security equipment and services to the government. The Central Intelligence Agency has established its own venture-capital arm, called In-Q-Tel, to help fund companies that are developing cutting-edge technologies for intelligence gathering. Major military contractors—Raytheon Company, The Boeing Company, and Lockheed Martin Corp., for example—are creating new marketing strategies for the fast-growing domestic security business, and the odds are that this new thrust will only get bigger. "The real windfall lies down the road," Phil Anderson, head of the homeland security initiative at the Washington-based Center for Strategic and International Studies, told the *Wall Street Journal*. "We're just seeing the tip of the iceberg."[16] There ought to be an ongoing assessment of these trends.

*How can the advisory council give adequate attention to
the international dimension of homeland security?*

As difficult as it may be to address the interdependencies of
America's domestic market, real security will be an illusion if
the global interdependencies are not addressed. For example,
the Centers for Disease Control (CDC) is developing a strategy
to counteract potential bioterrorism attacks in cooperation with
other countries since even an isolated instance of an infectious
disease can spread across borders with amazing speed. This
global mission for the CDC, though not completely new, will
need more attention and more resources and will require coordination from businesses and governments to an extent never
before envisioned. The prevention of agro-terrorism is another
area requiring cross-border collaboration. Were the food supply
to be contaminated with an infectious, disease-causing agent,
the disease could spread to U.S. trading partners or vice versa.
An adequate response would require an extensive and highly de-
centralized network of farmers, veterinarians, government officials, and agribusiness leaders. In the case of inspecting cargo
shipped by air or sea, the requirements for international cooperation are substantial, too.

Homeland security also compels a closer examination of the
vulnerability of the supply chains of American multinationals.
In the 1990s, their globalization strategies included locating and
consolidating manufacturing operations in the lowest-cost regions. By the beginning of the twenty-first century, the country
of choice was increasingly China. In the face of huge gaps in intelligence about China, the extent to which American manufacturing capability is vulnerable to a crisis in the Middle Kingdom
requires close examination. Investment has been pouring into
China at the expense of funds that used to go to other parts of
Asia and to Latin America. It is not just American firms that

have become infatuated with the Middle Kingdom; in the 1990s, Japan halved its investment in Southeast Asia and doubled it in China, and in 2000, Taiwan upped its investment in China five times over its 1999 investment. Companies like Intel, Dell, and Cisco have made huge bets on China, as have the auto companies. But we don't know the full extent of the web of subcontractors that are in China, because no such statistics have been gathered. Nor has there been any serious government analysis of the geographical concentration of these facilities in particular regions of China. We have no good sense of the contingency plans of America's manufacturers should a crisis arise—a war, terrorism, a natural disaster, or serious domestic unrest, for example. It's time for the United States to look at China, the world's manufacturing hub, with the same concerns it has in analyzing its dependence on Saudi Arabia for oil. And the United States should examine other parts of the world, such as regions in India, where a good deal of the world's software is being developed, for similar vulnerabilities.[17]

America's international interests are nowhere greater than in Mexico and Canada. When we think about homeland security, we ought to include the NAFTA region. To its credit, the Bush administration has taken several measures to enhance cooperation on the borders: The United States now shares with Canada visa information and other data on people crossing borders, and it has established a pilot program to pre-clear and expedite traffic coming from Canada. But the nation needs to do much more with its NAFTA partners to create an effective, common security zone that enhances rather than undercuts the massive trade flows between the three economics.

Homeland security, including the protection of critical infrastructure, presents the nation, the government, business leaders, and virtually every other element of society with what could be the biggest challenge of the next several decades. It will play a large role in the federal budget, in the organization of the government, in government-business relationships, and in the shaping of individual freedoms. In the end, the biggest challenge will be to enhance security without raising costs beyond what is absolutely necessary, without stifling innovation, without closing borders, and without undermining the freedoms that Americans cherish in a democratic, market-oriented system. The debate over how to do all this has just begun, and business leaders ought to be playing a major and constructive role in the design and implementation of national security at home.

CHAPTER 5

RESTORING INTEGRITY

TO MARKETS

T HE HISTORY OF American financial markets is punctu-
ated by recurrent scandals that shake the confidence of
investors. In the 1920s, Charles Ponzi defrauded some forty
thousand people of $15 million, a huge amount for the time. In
1930, Ivar Krueger, whose companies made two-thirds of the
world's matches, created four hundred off-the-books entries that
eventually caused the collapse of his empire. In 1961, executives
of GE, Westinghouse Electric Company, and other companies
were convicted of conspiring to rig bidding on federal projects. In
1986, investment bankers Ivan Boesky and Michael Milken
were jailed for market manipulation. This was followed by the sav-
ings-and-loan scandals (1989), health-care scams surrounding
Columbia/HCA (1997), and price fixing at Sotheby's and Christie's
auction houses (2000). These are but a few examples of serious
transgressions, but it is fair to say that throughout history, capitalism has often driven market participants to extremes.[1]

Despite the abundant historical scandals, the sheer scope of
those surrounding the Enron Corporation in 2002—including
the accounting irregularities of WorldCom, Global Crossing, and
Tyco, not to mention charges of malfeasance on the part of Arthur

Andersen itself—will be seen by historians as a watershed in the saga of American business. Congress, the Securities and Exchange Commission (SEC), and the Bush administration have all been deeply concerned with the deterioration of the integrity of America's capital markets. After Enron collapsed, they struggled to understand precisely how, within just a few months, one of the world's largest and most admired companies turned into the biggest corporate bankruptcy in American history. What was the role of Enron's top management and board of directors? How could auditors, analysts, credit agencies, underwriters, lenders, and regulators all have failed to see the debacle before it hit national headlines? What could be done to insure that the problems were effectively dealt with? In perhaps the first presidential address that ever detailed so many aspects of a financial problem, President Bush gave a speech on corporate governance and accounting. He was not alone in making policy proposals; they were coming out of the SEC, state regulators, the stock exchanges, Congress, the accounting profession, and even some business groups. Harvey Pitt, SEC chairman, was promising "the greatest overhaul in securities legislation since the SEC was created," ten congressional panels were focusing on the various problems, and over thirty bills were introduced to remedy them.[2]

The proposals fell into a number of categories. Some related to tighter standards for governance, accounting, and disclosure. Others dealt with allegedly distorted compensation incentives for CEOs, board members, and Wall Street analysts. Congress was tightening legal penalties for corporate misconduct, and investigating ways to protect workers' pensions when companies collapsed. There were demands for new regulatory agencies for accounting that would report to the SEC. Wall Street firms were pressured to prevent their analysts from manipulating their research to benefit their firm's business. *Business Week's* John Byrne summarized the crisis in public trust in business: "Faith in Corporate America hasn't been so strained since the early 1900s, when the public's furor over the monopoly powers of big business led to years of trust-busting by Theodore Roosevelt."[3]

Understandably, in this politically charged environment, very few business leaders spoke out. As noted in chapter 3, Goldman Sachs's chairman and CEO, Henry Paulson Jr., was one of the first to do so in a high-profile way, but all told, CEOs were generally quiet. Who among them would want to indict the system of which they were a principal part? Who among them would want to draw special attention to their own companies? In my off-the-record discussions with a variety of CEOs, however, many were clearly appalled. But I also had the impression that many believed that the storm would blow over as an economic recovery took hold and the stock market began to improve. These executives thought that the push for more regulation had an air of unreality about it. For example, many CEOs believed that the idea of elevating the responsibility of their boards of directors, though well intended, was supremely unpractical. In their view, directors could never know enough about the complex operations and accounts of global companies to take a larger role in oversight. One of three things—or possibly all of them—would happen: (1) The boards would attempt to micromanage a company, to the detriment of the firm; (2) the boards, fearful of liability, would hire their own counsel to advise them on a variety of company issues, thereby creating dysfunctional layers of advisers; or (3) the best board members would throw up their hands and resign, leaving the least qualified to govern.

In this context, business lobbying groups rallied to oppose restrictive legislation that would subject their clients to greater legal liability or would otherwise impose what they believed to be onerous regulation. In an election year, however, the legislators were under heavy pressure to show their constituents that they were taking firm and effective measures to deal with the

Enron spectacle. The outcome of this tug-of-war may take a year or two to emerge, but whatever Congress does, it will only be the beginning of the story. Legislation is likely to deal with only a few issues, and perhaps not even the major ones. New laws may well add to the mind-boggling complexity of auditing and reporting and create even more ways to make an end run around the legal rules. Congress itself may not be the principal arena of activity, either. The SEC, the Justice Department, the states' attorneys general, the stock exchanges—they will surely generate the bulk of new procedures. One thing is for sure: the scandals revealed deep cracks in the foundations of our markets.

American business scandals have usually unfolded in a predictable pattern. A transgression comes to light, accompanied by the drumbeat of sensational news stories. One or more bankruptcies are involved. This is followed by high-profile congressional hearings led by legislators who purport to be outraged, and by lengthy government investigations. Financial penalties and occasionally jail sentences are imposed, and eventually some new legislation is passed. By this time in the cycle, however, the market has generally moved on and public preoccupation is elsewhere, especially if the stock markets are rising again.

The trouble with this pattern of events is not what happens but what doesn't. The lessons learned are often obscured by the range and complexity of all that has taken place. The evidence that the original problems have been fixed is measured in terms of legislation, even though most people understand that a good deal of human behavior cannot be legislated. Nevertheless, in the wake of Enron and the wide range of abuses that have occurred, CEOs should improve on this process. They should deal constructively with the damage done to the reputation of American business culture and to public confidence in the integrity of the financial markets. This restored confidence would assure the public that a company's financial reports are accurate and meaningful and that business leaders and others who are critical to the investment community—such as Wall Street analysts— are acting honestly on behalf of an open and fair system. Business leaders need to create a thoughtful record of what went wrong and what the long-term business remedies are, not just to fix the problems but to educate future executives. This record ought to be simply written and widely distributed and debated in business circles and beyond.

AGENDA ITEM: THE ADMINISTRATION AND BUSINESS LEADERS SHOULD CONDUCT A POSTMORTEM OF RECENT SCANDALS, WITH RECOMMENDATIONS FOR STRENGTHENING AMERICA'S BUSINESS CULTURE

After the November 2002 midterm elections, CEOs should encourage President Bush to establish a special commission of business leaders—some recently retired and some active, as well as representatives of boards of directors—to provide their own analysis of what went wrong and what can be done. Top business executives will benefit from the establishment of this commission by playing a leadership role. Since it is their collective reputation that has suffered, it ought to be their objective to restore maximum integrity to the markets that are now so highly suspect. The group should include men and women from other arenas—labor and academia, for example—and representatives reflecting the interest of investors.

The commission should not be asked to identify people who transgressed the law or to propose new legislation; all this will or should be handled elsewhere. Nor should the commission start from scratch when other groups have already done thoughtful work. For example, the New York Stock Exchange has recommended a number of important measures to improve corporate governance. By the fall of 2002, the Conference Board will have delivered its report. SEC chairman Harvey Pitt has been increasingly aggressive in proposing corrective measures, too. In building on all this activity, the commission could start with the consensus that has been building on several fronts including the following: (1) Boards should have a majority of independent directors, and key committees—audit, compensation—should be composed entirely of independent directors. (2) The CEO and CFO must take personal responsibility for insuring that their financial accounts present an accurate picture of their company's business; they cannot use accountants and lawyers as a crutch. (3) CEO compensation needs to be reevaluated to be more consistent with the creation of long-term value. (4) Wall Street research analysts should not be paid according to the new business they bring in. (5) The accounting profession needs much more effective oversight.

In some of these areas, a variety of contending proposals have been made, and in some the ideas proposed are vague. So there is no lack of challenges for the commission. Moreover, in addition to looking at these specific issues, the commission should analyze the basic tenets of business culture that were trampled in the Enron and other scandals and articulate the concepts that ought to govern business behavior in the future. Here are some of the issues it should highlight:

Relieving Short-Term Earnings Pressures

The commission should analyze why CEOs find themselves under pressure to boost earnings each quarter and to set and precisely reach their targets no matter what the cost. It should examine the means of alleviating this relentless pressure so that creating long-term value is the prime goal and incentive of both the top executives and the directors. It would be important to document the profile of different classes of investors, including the proportion whose behavior is consistently short term or speculative in nature. The evidence may well show that it is not possible for CEOs to build and manage their companies for the long term, given how most shareholders behave, or how the most important ones, those who hold the most shares, behave. There could well be a need for a tax system that changes investor behavior, taxing short-term gains at a higher rate than now exists, and lowering or eliminating gains on shares held for several years.

The committee should look at changing the pattern of top-level corporate interaction with Wall Street analysts who demand that companies provide "earnings guidance," that is, a declaration of expected quarterly earnings. This pernicious ritual forces executives to gear all their actions—including playing games with how and when they book revenues and expenses—in order to precisely achieve what they "estimated." Put simply, chief executives should cease the practice of giving quarterly earnings guidance. If only a few CEOs abandoned the practice, they could be penalized by adverse publicity suggesting that they don't know enough about their firm's situation to make an estimate. To be sure, such behavior could be interpreted negatively by investors, who would sell the stock. But if business leaders abandoned the practice en masse, they could control the game. They would still discuss the future with analysts, but they would talk about a series of financial targets and longer-term goals for investments, return on capital, and strategic positioning. If, as a group, they have the courage to follow this course, corporate executives will help to change the short-term mindset of the markets.[4]

Strengthening Accounting Systems

The commission should recommend fundamental changes in the accounting system so that financial reporting is not just a matter of meeting the letter of the law but also a matter of presenting a clear and accurate picture of a company's business and its prospects. Several top figures in the accounting profession are calling for an overhaul, condemning the financial reporting system as too rigid and faulting it for measuring the past and not the present, and for not helping investors evaluate the future. Arguing that the current system is a relic of the industrial age, the critics say that the system doesn't take account of the new technological era, in which research, patents, and information technology are crucial to the evolution of most companies. They say the accounting rules have grown in volume and complexity, in the same way that the tax code has. "In the process, we have fostered a technical, legalistic mind-set that is sometimes more concerned with the form rather than the substance of what is reported," said Steven Butler, just before he retired as chairman of KPMG. "In our post-industrial economy, our accounting system doesn't do a very good job of describing any modern company."[5]

An international group in London has been working to establish international accounting standards (discussed later in this chapter). Besides taking a look at the standards that this group is proposing, the SEC should establish a group consisting of accountants, business leaders, lawyers, and investors to outline what financial reporting ought to look like a decade from now. Given the changes in the U.S. industrial structure, the special requirements of the information age, and the sorting and dissemination of investor information that new communications technology makes possible, undoubtedly financial reporting will become more complex than it currently is.

Also, the commission ought to take a hard look at the issue of disclosure of information. Everyone is for more and faster disclosure, but that solution is not a silver bullet. The fact is, most investors are overwhelmed with the volume and complexity of the information they already receive. They need less material, but content that is more fundamental to a company's performance, and written in plainer language. To this end, investors should hear from business executives about the information they and their staffs use to measure the value of their company and track those factors that are driving that value. This is basic information that the public needs before it is buried in reams of technical data that few can comprehend. Yet, with companies like GE promising to produce annual reports the size of telephone books to meet the perceived demands for disclosure of information, investors will be more confused than ever.

Reining in Executive Compensation

The commission should analyze executive compensation and the behavior it encourages. Few Americans would argue that CEOs should not be rewarded for a company's outstanding performance, but most are sure to object to rewarding them when performance is poor. Yet in April 2002 several analyses of executive compensation showed that the total compensation of many chief executives rose even as their company's performance deteriorated. In virtually every case the reason could be attributed to sizable allotments of stock options. To be sure, the accurate calculation of remuneration is often more complicated than the media indicate. Options packages are issued in a way that usually permits their being exercised for a ten-year period, whereas the actual markets for trading options are much shorter term. Some formulas assign a value in the absence of real market prices, but they are highly imperfect. Nevertheless, in the 1990s, stock options were being awarded as if they were free, and by 2002 they constituted 75 percent of top executive compensation. Particularly egregious was the technique of allowing CEOs to swap their out-of-the-money, high-priced options for lower ones—something not available to shareholders or ordinary employees. Roy Smith and Ingo Walter, professors at the Stern School of Business at New York University, described the inappropriate compensation of executives: "The methods used to reward management have become absurd. They are paid to sign up, paid to stay, even paid to go—often at eye-popping rates that bear no relation to the results achieved."[6]

All the questions surrounding stock options—the amounts awarded, the way they are accounted for, the performance criteria on which they are based—must be reexamined. Options cost a company nothing, since it need not deduct them as an expense, as it must do for most other kinds of compensation, but they are a tax deduction when they can be ultimately exercised. The people who do pay are the shareholders, whose holdings are diluted when the options are converted into stock. It is understandable why corporate America embraces stock options with such enthusiasm. CEOs themselves can acquire enormous wealth. Options can effectively motivate a manager to work toward an increase in a company's stock price, thereby aligning the interest of management with shareholders. (One must ask, however, which shareholders—the speculators or those interested in the long term?) In addition, treating options as an expense would reduce the earnings of virtually every major publicly listed company. (The Federal Reserve estimates that between 1995 and 2000, if the Standard & Poor's 500 companies had accounted for their options as an expense, their average annual earnings growth would have declined from 12 percent to 9.4 percent.) But these are not reasons to ignore what should be done in the interest of accurate accounting, proper alignment of incentives, and basic fairness. Warren Buffett poses these questions: "If options aren't a form of compensation, what are they? If compensation isn't an expense, what is it? And, if expenses shouldn't go into calculations of earnings, where in the world should they go?" He was once a lone voice, but others have now joined him—including Federal Reserve chairman Alan Greenspan and former chairman Paul Volcker. Says Sarah Teslik, executive director of the Council of Institutional Investors, "[Unexpensed options] turn companies into Ponzi schemes."[7]

A postmortem on the Enron era must come to grips with the sheer magnitude of unexpensed options, which are creating perverse incentives, driving CEOs and top management to push the envelope to drive up stock prices in the short term. It would be far better to report the options as an expense, at least when they are exercised (when the true value can be determined), and to issue them in far smaller quantities. Moreover, stock options should not reward CEOs just because the overall stock market is rising but only when the stock appreciation outstrips those of their peer companies as well as an index of stocks over a period of, say, three years. Similarly important, quarterly financial reports should clearly describe a company's total exposure to outstanding options—not just to those held by top management —and the potential impact on the value of the existing shareholders' stocks when the options are exercised. Better still, CEOs and other top executives should be rewarded with actual stock that can be sold only over a long time. This would insure that their interests are aligned with those shareholders who are also interested in the creation of value not just for this quarter, but for many more to come.

These arguments are not new and have many permutations, some of which are being vigorously debated in Congress, the SEC, and the media. It is perhaps a stretch to believe that business executives themselves would work with Congress on some of these alternatives for more equitable executive compensation. Presently, the investing public has little confidence that top executives are not out merely to enrich themselves, and very lavishly at that. According to calculations at *Business Week,* for example, in 1980 CEO compensation was 42 times that of the average worker, whereas in 2000 it was 531 times the average.[8] Still, were some CEOs to take the lead on establishing a better system for executive compensation, it would be the right thing to do—the public-interest thing to do—and if a handful of America's top leaders spoke up together, they could have significant influence.

Rethinking the Role of Boards of Directors

The commission should discuss the full obligations of boards of directors in the future. It should pay attention to the independence of the board, the qualifications for membership, and the means of compensating directors so as to insure a longer-term perspective. These questions have been debated in the SEC as well as in the stock exchanges and academic institutions, but what makes the situation different today is the sheer difficulty of overseeing big companies in complex global markets.

The commission ought to give serious attention to a proposal made to elevate corporate governance standards. In April 2002, John C. Whitehead, former chairman of Goldman Sachs, and Ira M. Millstein, senior partner of Weil, Gotshal & Manges, LLP, a law firm in New York, advocated that the SEC establish a national code of conduct for boards of directors, something that does not now exist. Although companies would not be obligated to follow all the guidelines, they would be required to provide an explanation of where they chose not to, and why. The Whitehead-Millstein proposal echoes others that go in a similar direction, and it is an idea whose time has come. The proposal itself doesn't explain the specific standards to be followed, but here are some of the most important categories: defining the meaning of "independent" director; defining the precise relationship between directors and outside audit committees; defining whether directors should be paid in cash, stock options, or stock; defining whether there should be a separation between the chairman of the board, who would be an independent director, and the CEO.[9]

The commission should also raise other issues. Beyond vouching for the financial position of a company, and beyond hiring, firing, and determining the compensation of the CEO and other top management, to what degree should directors become involved in the strategy of a company, particularly in public policy issues, such as domestic and foreign environmental and labor policies? Most executives I know would vehemently oppose such an extension of the board's role. Their argument is that directors are part-timers with insufficient knowledge of a company's situation and capabilities. True enough. But there is another view, too. CEOs—particularly those of large, complex multinationals—are no longer in a position to handle all their internal and external responsibilities. They need help; they need networks of colleagues who are not mired in the day-to-day operations of their companies, people who can evaluate the context for a variety of decisions that, if they go wrong, could severely damage a company's brand. Who better to play this role than a company's independent directors? These are controversial issues that will not be addressed by Congress or the SEC in the blizzard of Enron-related reactions. But as part of a postmortem, they should be.

Reassessing the Role of Institutional Investors

The commission should take a hard look at the role that big institutional investors play in our financial markets. These institutions could play a pivotal role in upgrading corporate governance, were they so inclined. At the beginning of 2001, for example, mutual funds controlled by the seventy largest fund managers owned $2.9 trillion of U.S. publicly listed equity, 20 percent of the entire market capitalization. If the value of the pension funds and other institutions whose funds are controlled by these managers are combined, their total voting power would reflect the 44 percent of the shares they own.[10]

Are these institutions up to the challenge? Says John Bogle, founder and former chairman of the Vanguard Group of mutual funds, "The record shows only sparse attention to corporate governance issues by [these institutions]."[11] Nevertheless, he is a strong advocate for a more proactive stance on the part of the big funds. In June 2002, there appeared to be additional momentum on the part of leading institutional investors as the International Corporate Governance Network, a global organization of pension funds that controls $10 trillion of assets around the world, was gearing up to establish guidelines for corporate governance of the companies in which they invest.[12] The commission ought to give this overall movement a big push.

Reviewing Business Culture Itself

The commission should take a look at America's deteriorating business culture itself, with the goal of recommending ways to improve the climate. What is required is no less than an explanation of how and why trust and integrity deteriorated so badly in the 1980s and 1990s. This is not a call for a broad indictment, for the United States and the rest of the world greatly benefited from the incredible burst of technological innovation that CEOs largely led during this period. But along the way, business lost any sense of a moral compass. Companies became just bundles of assets to be bought and sold. Employees became commodities to be hired and fired. The very notion of what constituted real value in the new economy was conflated with getting bigger and moving faster—but not with profitability, not with the welfare of employees, not with the development of communities. How did this happen? What can be done to prevent a recurrence?

One major issue of integrity that needs examination is the notion of conflict of interest in modern, complex markets. The clearest recent transgressions are instances in which Wall Street analysts recommended stocks to help their firms get other business from firms that benefited by the analysts' "buy" recommendations. The CEOs of these investment banks—indeed, a good deal of the investment community—were complicit in this charade. But this wasn't the end of conflicts of interest. Investment banks issued scarce shares in new initial public offerings to favored clients in return for new business. Auditors performed consulting work for clients, work that was often more lucrative than the auditing itself. Directors compromised themselves by having financial relationships—over and above their board compensation—with the firm on whose board they served. Governmental regulators came from the industries they now oversee, and to which they were destined to return when their government service ended. All this was reinforced by a new-economy business culture in which many of the familiar lines that separated activities and businesses seemed to disappear. The buzzwords—"convergence," "virtual companies," "centerless corporations"—said it all. Companies formed partnerships with their customers and their competitors. The emergence of big conglomerates like GE, Citigroup, and AOL Time Warner was in part an effort to facilitate cross-selling of products of one division to the customers of another. Lawyers and consultants invested in their clients. The distinctions between companies engaged in finance, technology, and communications became blurred. It's no wonder that executives lost a sense of moral direction.

It is easy to say that business leaders should do the right thing. But doing the right thing is not that simple. If an activity is legal, then is it automatically right? If there is no law prohibiting a certain action, then is it OK to do? We live in an environment in which the tyranny of Wall Street's pressure on short-term results drives so much, in which accounting rules are subject to a wide range of legitimate interpretation, in which regulations are in flux—indeed, in which the world is moving quickly and unevenly from an industrial to an information age. In this environment, there is no substitute for reasoned judgment that takes account of the broadest array of factors in addition to the law. The executives most capable of such behavior will put the highest premium on who they surround themselves with, how they get their information, and how open they are to challenges by their colleagues. These executives will be concerned not just with winning a deal, but with *how* they win it.

Another aspect of trust and integrity concerns this question: If some employees in a firm transgress the law or internal ethical standards, are both the firm and the CEO themselves culpable? In a world in which companies have been consolidating via mergers or a mind-boggling array of strategic alliances, the question of who bears the responsibility for the parts or subparts of a multifaceted organization is of no small consequence. Top officials at Arthur Andersen alleged that the entire company should not be punished just because a few of them shredded documents. At Merrill Lynch, chairman and CEO David Komansky admitted that some stock analysts violated the firm's standards, but he said he did not think it was fair to point a finger at the eight hundred professionals in Merrill's research department.[13] He later told CNBC that, as CEO, "Anything that happens on my watch I'm responsible for."[14] But it's not clear what these statements add up to. Who is properly accountable, and who should bear not just the blame but the punishment?

Although a CEO cannot know everything that is going on in a huge multinational company, the top management is responsible for the culture of the company and its organizational systems of checks and balances. In the case of accounting and financial firms, if brand name doesn't stand for reliability and integrity throughout all its products and services, then exactly what does it represent? James O'Toole of the University of California explains that an organization must pay a heavy price when one part violates the public trust. Otherwise, he says, "other organizations have no incentive to be vigilant; nor are employees at all levels motivated to demand adherence to stated corporate values and standards of conduct. . . . In the end the issue is one of organizational accountability." [15]

The importance of a national discussion about business behavior is this: Without character and trust in our markets, we will fall back on more laws, more regulations, more audits—and audits of audits. There could be so much disclosure of information that no one will be able to determine what's really important. We cannot legislate ethical business behavior, but it can be reinforced in many subtle and important ways. American presidents bestow the Baldrige Award to companies that demonstrate the highest quality of products and services. Why not similar accolades for business leaders of character? The media fixates on CEOs whose share prices soar; why not give more attention to those whose ethical values are models for others? These and similar suggestions no doubt sound mundane, mechanical, and perhaps Pollyanna-ish. A commission looking into possibilities for promoting more integrity in the business culture may have much better ideas. But the essential point should not be lost: The more complex the markets become, the more the integrity of its leaders matters, and the less likely that higher prescriptive laws and regulations will really matter.

Connecting Domestic and Foreign Business Behavior

The commission should examine how the reforms taking place in the United States interact with the framework for auditing and corporate governance abroad. The shares of numerous foreign companies are listed on the U.S. exchanges, and many American corporations issue their shares abroad. Foreign companies ought to be under the same pressures to disclose information and otherwise govern themselves as do American firms.

Take just one example. Today you can buy shares of several Chinese companies on the New York Stock Exchange, yet in China the tradition of independent directors on companies' boards doesn't exist. From the perspective of American investors, who then is minding the store with regard to these Chinese entities? Who should be minding it, and how should they be doing so?

In fact, the international issue of corporate governance ought to loom very large in the post-Enron agenda. In a global economy, multinational companies ought to be managed according to some common standards. Very often in the past, the United States arrogantly assumed that its standards of corporate governance—including its accounting standards—were so superior that the rest of the world needed to adopt American techniques, and that the United States had nothing to learn from others. Now that the Enron and Arthur Andersen debacles have revealed problems in the American system, the United States can—and must—work with other countries to come up with global standards.

One place to begin would be with the accounting system. What, after all, could be more fundamental than having a single financial language for global business? Yet such a universal language doesn't exist; the United States uses one system, and European countries use different methodologies, as does Japan. Since 1993 the International Accounting Standards Board, an international group based in London, has been trying to develop one set of rules that everyone can use. It is time for the United States to put its full weight behind this search for one system that companies can use and investors can understand. Unlike the American system, it should be simpler and more comprehensible to nonspecialists. It should have a clear business purpose, not just a legal justification. An international system must not represent a dilution of U.S. standards but must stand for the highest common denominator of what exists around the world. Moreover, where there are gaps, international standard setters ought to move quickly to fill them.

Beyond working on business accounting standards, the commission should give attention to the movement for improving corporate governance in Russia, China, and other countries. As the United States improves its own system, it should be working with the public and private sectors elsewhere to improve theirs. Poor corporate governance abroad increases the likelihood of corruption, slow growth, and financial crises that can easily spill over borders. The American business community could take a number of actions. As the New York Stock Exchange and the NASDAQ exchange proceed to upgrade the corporate governance standards for their members, they should work with their counterparts in London, Frankfurt, Hong Kong, and Tokyo to press for higher governance standards for all companies. Standard & Poor's and Moody's Investors Service should develop metrics to evaluate corporate governance practices in all international companies and include them in their credit ratings. The Big Five accounting firms, with SEC encouragement, should be working with regulatory authorities and clients around the world to tighten auditing procedures. Regulators of global financial institutions should enforce common governance principles, given that the activities of these banking-brokerage-insurance Goliaths are so pivotal to the health of the global economy. All aspects of corporate governance must be considered in a global context.

The Enron debacle ought to usher in a new era of corporate governance in general. American business leaders will find that a thoughtful assessment of the new business environment and the required new standards will be a difficult and painful exercise. But if CEOs abdicate this assessment by default to Congress, the administration, and regulators, then they will invite new government intrusions that meet the public clamor to do something, but that will inevitably include overregulation. "We have to be careful not to look at a significant expansion of regulation as the solution to our problems," said Alan Greenspan.[16] Of course, there is another scenario, too, one in which government does very little to respond to the corporate crisis, because it is paralyzed or distracted by other issues. This outcome would also be unfortunate, since the transgressions that have damaged America's companies, markets, and investors will go unattended. There is a crying need for leadership, and the people who ought to provide it should come from the best of the corporate world.

CHAPTER 6

PRESERVING

ECONOMIC SECURITY

C ONTRIBUTING TO THE RESPONSE to terrorism and to
the restoration of confidence in U.S. markets are relatively new on the CEO public-policy agenda. But there are knotty,
long-standing problems that business leaders should also focus
on to strengthen the bonds of society that September 11 and
Enron have undermined. These problems include health care and
Social Security, both of which require added attention in light of
the nation's newly strained public finances.

Admittedly, many of us find that our eyes glaze over when
these issues come up. But this doesn't mean they are not critically important. And in the context of the post–September 11,
post-Enron environment, there are a number of issues that
should compel leaders from business, government, and the not-
for-profit sector to be concerned. First of all, the cost of the war
on terrorism is escalating rapidly, crowding out many domestic
social programs. The budgets for traditional defense and for
homeland security have become essentially nonnegotiable from
a political standpoint, too. In addition, the "Enron effect" has
helped to lower corporate valuations and slow trading and investing in the stock markets, and it has therefore reduced the
revenues that federal and state governments were getting from

taxes on capital gains. Second, the erosion of public trust in the corporate world risks being further eviscerated if companies cannot provide opportunity for reasonable health care at affordable prices. And the same erosion will apply to the government if it welches on its perceived commitments to long-term Social Security. In other words, Americans are understandably on edge about their physical security and their financial security, and if the broad social contract is broken in addition, no one should be surprised if an upheaval in politics, characterized by deep disenchantment with the current state of affairs, ensues.

Since the days of the Committee on Economic Development, CEOs have voiced their views about fiscal policy, and many have had some involvement in the health care and Social Security issues. Much of this activity, however, has centered on lobbying efforts for or against one plan or another. Business executives should play a more elevated role, looking at the federal budget not just for tax breaks or provisions that benefit their particular company or industry but for the longer-term impact of the budget on the country's economy and its citizens. The United States needs constructive business leadership in the debates on guns versus butter, on the effects of surpluses and deficits on the domestic and international economy, and on the financing of key social programs, including those of an aging society. In these arenas, as in others, corporate executives will need to team up with experts from other fields, including top economists. But the CEOs should not hesitate to play a leading role in the effort.

AGENDA ITEM: CEOS SHOULD HELP
RESTORE FISCAL SOUNDNESS

Not only has the nation moved from fiscal surpluses to deficits, but it has lost control of fiscal policy. In January 2001, the Congressional

Budget Office (CBO) predicted a cumulative budget surplus of $5.6 trillion between 2002 and 2011.[1] At the beginning of 2002, that number had fallen to $1.6 trillion; in other words, $4 trillion had evaporated. The CBO attributed 60 percent of the decrease to the president's tax-reduction initiative of 2001, and 40 percent to what was then considered a recession. But the projected $1.6 trillion surplus did not take into account additional expenditures for military modernization, the war on terrorism, further tax breaks that the administration is likely to advocate, or any substantial new domestic or international programs. No sooner were these projections published than they were overtaken by President Bush's proposals later in the month to fund the largest military buildup since the Reagan years and vastly expanded outlays for homeland security. On the military side, the president requested funds for both the costs of combating terrorism and a general upgrade of the military—higher pay, more planes and tanks, research on a national missile defense system. The president also requested more money for border security, emergency response, public health, and the protection of information technology. All the while, he was emphasizing that the war had just begun and that the dangers were escalating beyond anything the nation had previously contemplated: "Whatever it costs to defend our nation, we will pay."[2] Consequently, in March 2002, the CBO again reduced its projection: Instead of $1.6 trillion, the CBO said the new surplus over the next ten years would be slightly less than $1 trillion. But even this wasn't the end of the story. In April 2002, President Bush asked Congress to make his $1.35 trillion tax cut permanent, as opposed to the original ten-year plan. The *New York Times* estimated that the proposal would drain $400 billion from the budget between 2002 and 2010, and another $4 trillion between 2010 and 2020: "A more irresponsible position would be hard to imagine," it said in an editorial.[3]

Who can argue with a strong defense at home and abroad? But in their patriotism and zeal for preparedness, Americans shouldn't be blind to the fiscal debacle shaping up. For several reasons, the budget before Congress could now grossly understate the magnitude of future deficits. In the late 1980s and early 1990s, legal restraints compelled Congress to offset any increased discretionary spending in one area with cuts in another, but these restraints are no longer in force. Also, the current budget includes no provisions for Social Security reform, a prime objective of the administration. To illustrate what a dire situation we are in, it is worth remembering that early in this century aging baby boomers will drain public expenditures for Social Security and health care, and a prudent nation would be preparing now by building up a surplus.

The United States will face other serious problems unless it returns not just to a balanced fiscal situation but to one of substantial surpluses. The first consequence would be an evisceration of the domestic social agenda, as military and homeland-security expenses soar. From 1987 to 2002, defense spending as a proportion of gross domestic product declined from 7 to 4 percent. As it moves back up—and it is impossible to tell how far it will go, since Congress often increases whatever the president and even the military itself ask for—health care and Social Security reform will be squeezed. The Social Security surplus will be used for general government operations, and the nation will have little money left to pay down the soaring national debt. When the financial strains on state and local governments are factored in—as these governments, too, face declining tax revenues and rising homeland-security costs—the potential problems are even more serious. Most states are legally bound to balance their budgets and therefore have no choice but to cut medical, unemployment compensation, and educational programs, as well as other investments.

A second consequence of out-of-control deficits is that they could force up long-term interest rates, as the public sector expands its borrowing and competes with business for funding. In addition, the evolving fiscal situation is reminiscent of the late 1980s, when rising budget deficits, trade deficits (which are also increasing now), and heavy American government borrowing from abroad led to international economic turmoil—and eventually the stock market crash of 1987. Today the situation is made unusually precarious, considering the widespread concerns about the stability of the dollar in global markets. Given the dominant position of the United States in the world economy, when its accounts are so far out of balance, trouble in international markets may not be far behind.

Finally, the deficits will create a bitter political environment similar to those during the mid-1980s to the mid-1990s, when the two political parties struggled over scarce resources and spent most of their time blaming each other, instead of passing important legislation. This battle will color everything else in Washington, including rational planning for homeland security and the strengthening of financial regulatory agencies.

In its June 2002 report on fiscal responsibility, The Concord Coalition, a public-interest group drawn from business, labor, and nonprofit institutions, provided a devastating analysis of the budgetary situation. "It is now clear that the appropriate loosening of fiscal policy undertaken in response to the mild recession and devastating attacks of 2001 is turning into a headlong retreat from long-term fiscal responsibility," it warned. "Indeed, the attitude seems to be if deficits are back, let's make the most of them and blame someone else for the result."[4]

To date, most business leaders have not participated in attempts to stem the deterioration of the nation's budget. It would be a powerful change of direction if top business executives initiated an effort to think through and advocate measures addressing the nation's long-term budget policy. If they could marshal efforts the way the Committee on Economic Development did in the

1940s and 1950s, CEOs would rail against Washington's attempts to placate every special-interest group—including business itself. Corporate leaders would fashion a conceptual framework for economic growth over the next decade and the monetary and fiscal policies that would underlie it. CEOs would be particularly sensitive to the implications of American financial imbalances in an increasingly integrated global economy. They might propose, as Alan Greenspan has, budgetary rules that make tax cuts and spending levels contingent on the size of the overall budget deficit or surplus—or at least establish some equally powerful guidelines for policy to replace what is now a strategic vacuum.

The big question is how to increase and exploit the long-term growth potential of the American economy. Should the government do it by lowering taxes to stimulate economic activity, which in turn will result in the added tax revenues needed to fund essential programs? Or should the government keep the money to make direct investments in the nation's productivity? The truth lies in some combination of tax relief and judicious spending, of course, but where on the spectrum? Another crucial question is how to reconcile the imperative of continued economic growth with the costs of enhanced homeland defense. To what degree will these new national security expenses cut into corporate profitability? To what extent should the government share the costs? As of 2002, the country lacks an agreed-upon philosophical and strategic framework for fiscal policy. Business leaders ought to be helping to develop one.

AGENDA ITEM: CEOS SHOULD HELP STRENGTHEN THE SOCIAL SAFETY NET

Fiscal policy is part of the security equation because it is central to the viability of America's social safety net. Consider health care. This is a social issue, of course, but it is also critical to the business community, since employers pay a major portion of the national health-care bill on behalf of their employees. Moreover, an effective health-care system is critical to the morale of the national work force and hence to its productivity. Big strains are appearing in this system, and part of their alleviation will depend on the extent to which employers continue to subsidize health care, and how they choose to do it.

In the early 1990s, 14 percent of Americans were uninsured. Although the percentage was the same in 2002, more people— nearly 40 million of them—are at risk. Even for those who are covered, health-care costs increased by almost 50 percent from 1997 to 2002. In 2000, total spending on health increased 6.9 percent to $1.3 trillion, the largest one year percentage increase since 1993. In addition, the two largest programs, Medicare and Medicaid, are being squeezed as government budgets go into the red. For 2002, for example, Medicare payments to doctors have been cut by over 5 percent. The result is that some physicians are strictly limiting the number of Medicare patients they see, and some 17 percent of family doctors are not taking new Medicare patients at all. The problem is exceptionally acute when it comes to the affordability of prescription drugs. In 2000, spending on such medications was up 19 percent; in 2001 it increased 17 percent. It's no wonder that this problem has become a political hot button in Washington every year. Looking to the period between 2003 and 2008, companies are facing average increases in health-care costs of 12 to 15 percent, with the strong likelihood that companies will cut back on the plans they offer employees or shift the cost to them.[5]

In this era of low inflation and hypercompetition, companies cannot pass the higher costs on to their customers; thus the employees must bear the burden, and at a time when slower growth has made their jobs more insecure. Doing so, however, will eventually backfire as health problems undercut productivity or as employers are forced to raise salaries to compensate for higher costs of health insurance. In the extreme—or maybe it's not so extreme a possibility—government would have to raise taxes to subsidize health care, thereby putting more burdens on an economy that now has more than its share. The pressures on health care are also mounting just as the U.S. government will have to make heavy new investments in public health to deal with potential bioterrorism. At the same time, the government needs to be preparing to care for an aging population, whose medical needs will be rising dramatically. "The American system of medicine is threatened with a meltdown," writes *Washington Post* columnist David Broder. "Tinkering around the edges cannot, for long, withstand the adverse trends, let alone reverse them. This is an issue that cannot wait for the war on terrorism to end."[6]

What can business leaders do? For starters they could put more pressure on health-care plans to be cost-efficient. They could, for example, demand more transparency about true costs. They could put more effort into evaluating plans for their employees, thereby creating more effective competition among plans. Large companies could allows smaller ones to join their health-care systems, so that the latter's employees could be better serviced.

The Midwestern Business Group on Health, comprising Ford, General Motors, DaimlerChrysler, and others, illustrates a complementary approach. It has applied advanced quality-control measures—the kind its own corporate members use in their companies—on hospitals. This includes computerized drug ordering to reduce errors that result from doctors' poor handwriting; setting and monitoring targets for medical errors; analyzing failures more rigorously—in short, applying a kind of Six Sigma approach (a highly elaborate quality-control procedure made famous by GE) to medical care.[7]

This is the tip of the iceberg of what companies can do, in addition to helping government think through the bigger policy issues.

The Social Security system is another big problem central to business and needing innovative solutions. In mid-2001, President Bush established a commission to come up with alternatives for keeping the system solvent well into this century, under the pressure of more retirees and fewer workers to finance them. The administration was keen to find ways to privatize at least part of Social Security by allowing citizens to have their own accounts, which they could invest in the stock market or elsewhere. In December 2001, the commission delivered its view of the alternative solutions, all woefully incomplete. You can allow people to have their private accounts, it said, as long as you make some major structural changes. These changes include policies like massive government subsidies or large cutbacks in benefits—something to offset an estimated $1 trillion to $3 trillion in transition costs to a new system, costs that are incurred when the Social Security taxes of workers are no longer available to pay for retirees, but are instead invested in those workers' own savings accounts. Cutting back dramatically on benefits is a political nonstarter. And because of upcoming budget deficits, money for gigantic subsidies is not in sight. Indeed, in the president's budget for 2002–2003, Social Security surpluses are slated to pay for other government programs through 2013, a policy that could ultimately siphon off $1.4 trillion from Social Security funds. Not long ago, both Democrats and Republicans promised that this would never happen. "For years, politicians in both parties have dipped into the trust fund to pay for more spending—and I will stop it," said George W. Bush during his presidential campaign.[8] The words sound hollow now, especially in the aftermath of the Bush commission's conclusions. "[The commission's] final report declared that private accounts would indeed strengthen Social Security, if they were accompanied by sharp benefit cuts and huge financial injections from unspecified sources," wrote *New York Times* columnist Paul Krugman. "Yes, and eating a jelly doughnut every morning will help you lose weight, if you also cut back on other foods and do a lot of exercise."[9] In other words, the national debate over Social Security has gone nowhere, and the United States is still in dire need of a policy framework.

Business leaders ought to be pressing government not to put Social Security on the back burner and not to make proposals that are practical nonstarters. In the past, there was a sensible solution to the Social Security issue. A government-business commission was established, chaired by Alan Greenspan before he became Fed chairman. Both parties in Congress could nominate members, as could the administration. Both political parties agreed in advance to abide by the commission's recommendations. It was a triumph of public policy, even if it was clear that the "solution" would take the country through the next few decades before another fix would be required. That's a lot better than the non-approach that now exists.

A related issue is the changing pension system in the United States and the requirement for business leaders, among others, to take a hard look at the vulnerabilities building up. As noted in chapter 3, in the past, most Americans received pensions from their employers in the form of guaranteed payouts—so-called "defined benefit plans." Your pension was, in other words, an entitlement your employer paid once you worked at a company for a predetermined number of years. Today, however, in place of this kind of retirement benefit, companies have sponsored programs that allow employees to invest their own money—"defined contribution plans." These investments have become the primary retirement savings vehicles. They include 401(k) and profit-sharing and stock-bonus plans—none of which provide any guaranteed benefit or federal insurance to protect employees if a company goes bankrupt. Roughly 75 percent of all money invested in corporate retirement now goes into 401(k) plans. The way this retirement system is evolving poses a number of problems, some of them underscored by the big losses incurred by Enron employees.[10]

In the first place, these new plans came into existence in the early to mid-1980s, just as the stock market was beginning its eighteen-year boom. The future is likely to show much poorer market performance, reducing retirement payouts substantially. Another problem is the low overall savings rate in the United States, which means that many employees are probably fooling themselves into believing that they are saving enough for retirement. The insufficient education of the public about prudent investing presents a dangerous situation, given that so many lives now depend on knowledge of the market.

Business leaders favor the current system because it relieves them of the costs of managing pensions and paying them out, and it is far less costly in terms of their fixed obligations. Today companies pay less than 50 percent toward what employees themselves save. But despite these benefits to companies, the privatization of retirement is worrisome. Business should work with government to see how the longer-term foundation of this system can be strengthened. Any reforms that respond only to the problems exhibited in the Enron case would only be a small part of the picture. Providing incentives for greater saving and educating employees to make informed investment decisions are some other fundamental challenges.

The health care, Social Security, and broader retirement questions cannot be put aside for the antiterrorism campaign, because ultimately a sense of personal security needs to be seen holistically. A population insecure in an arena that affects its daily lives is going to be less interested in, and supportive of, other security projects. Practical input from CEOs would be an improvement on the ideological debates taking place in Congress on the subject. Of particular value would be the input of a high-level group, driven by business, to tackle the big challenges. What are the requirements for a secure work force in a rapidly changing global economy? What constitutes a twenty-first-century social safety net? How can the public and private sectors work together to achieve these goals? These issues must be part of the new agenda for business leaders.

CHAPTER 7

SUSTAINING FREE TRADE

IN THE 1980S AND 1990S, international trade and investment expanded at phenomenal rates. World trade grew by about 84 percent; investment across borders increased even more. Although we can't measure precisely the spread of new technologies, it is obvious that these, too, traveled almost as if there existed just one seamless, global market. In these past two decades, most governments dropped barriers to international commerce as fast as possible and businesses rushed to expand their operations to all corners of the world. Not surprisingly, the intensified globalization provoked political controversy. Not all countries and not all groups within them were benefiting equally. China and Mexico prospered, but regions like Africa and parts of the Middle East continued to stagnate. Many workers and their families lost their jobs to foreign competition or were displaced by new technology imported from abroad.

Critics saw global companies as powerful, unregulated organizations shaping the world according to their own mercenary designs. Multinational companies were accused of exploiting workers in poor countries and degrading the environment. The free market had run amok, some critics said, because there were inadequate mechanisms to regulate global business. Even many who championed the spread of capitalism were uneasy about the world economy's weak foundations. For them, the Asian financial crisis of 1997–1998 was a clear warning that even the most sophisticated emerging markets needed stronger regulatory structures. In Asia and Latin America, government leaders and economists were questioning the free-market policies of the International Monetary Fund, The World Bank, and the U.S. Treasury. The antiglobal protests that had their start in Seattle supplied further evidence that balancing free markets and regulation would become a daunting economic and political challenge.

No one can know for sure how globalization will play out, but we can imagine the scenarios at either end of a spectrum of possibilities. The first is a rough extrapolation of what has already taken place: a steady increase in global trade and investment across the globe, stimulated by a continuing drop in trade barriers and the deregulation of industries within individual countries. There will be heated political controversies and recurrent financial crises. Efforts to build stronger foundations for the world economy will continue, although the process will take a long time. Despite political tensions in many parts of the world, the center will hold, and in some messy way, U.S.-European relations—the linchpin of the global economy—will remain strong. Furthermore, negotiations with the developing world will include compromises and other settlements. This scenario assumes that the underlying forces of global economic integration are simply too powerful to be stopped.

The other extreme is a precipitous slowdown in globalization. Nationalism will have won the day. Trade and foreign investment will not stop, but the intense momentum will have dissipated. The tightening of borders and the new regulations accompanying the worldwide fight against terrorism will counteract efforts to further open the international economy. A gradual but noticeable rise in protectionism will take place, led by escalating trade tensions between the United States and Europe over export subsidies, steel, agriculture, bioengineered food, privacy, and so forth. Added to transatlantic tensions will be fundamental differences over foreign policy in the Middle East and in the war against terrorism more generally. Whole regions of the world, such as the Islamic countries between Morocco and Saudi Arabia, will be engulfed in political turmoil; other areas, like most of southern Africa, will effectively drop out of the global economy under the weight of their abject miseries. Regionalism will be a more powerful force than globalism, and we will see more political energy applied to building ties within Europe, within the Arab world, within Latin America, rather than applied to global agreements. Many more countries will refuse to follow policy prescriptions designed in Washington and on Wall Street. There will be a strong tilt toward local politics and culture and away from global integration.

What makes the present moment so important is that our response to the terrorist attacks of September 11 and to the Enron debacle will have a lot to do with which scenario prevails. Without a concerted effort to combat certain trends, the combined impact of these two events will be to strongly reinforce the second scenario—the one that translates into an enormous setback in the momentum for a more open world economy.

Terrorism has pushed national security concerns to the top of the American agenda and lowered the priority of everything else, including government attempts to strengthen the world economy. The Bush administration may point to its efforts for global trade negotiations and expanded foreign aid as evidence to the contrary. No administration, however, no matter how skillful, can wage a global war and have much time and energy for other big projects requiring substantial diplomacy and resources. And many imperatives in the war on terrorism work against what the

United States would be doing if a strong global economy were its number one priority.

To begin with, terrorism creates a mind-set about globalization that is radically different from what we have known. Until September 11, globalization was synonymous with openness— with lowering trade barriers, encouraging more foreign investment, deregulating whole industries, privatizing firms. After the terrorist attacks, the new thrust is to "plug the holes" in the system so that the same channels that allowed the ever-freer flow of money, people, and technology do not become the channels that Al Qaeda and other terrorist groups utilize to penetrate society. Globalization was once synonymous with new markets and new opportunities for investors, entrepreneurs, and consumers; now there is at least equal concern about the vulnerabilities that come with the interdependence of our societies. Governments around the world have already evidenced this new way of thinking. Instead of stepping out of the way of free markets, they are returning in force. Instead of the "gradual withering of the state"—a faintly utopian theory that most parts of the world were beginning to embrace up until September 11—governments are cooperating with each other to clamp down in such areas as cross-border traffic in money and people. Terrorism has also undermined economic confidence by creating apprehension about the security of supply chains and adding to the costs of companies' operations. It has caused global firms to reassess where their operations are located, how they are organized, who their partners ought to be, and how they relate to foreign governments.

Enron and other corporate scandals have had a negative impact on globalization, too. Forces originating in the United States heavily influence the world economy, and there has been considerable overlap between globalization and "Americanization." The United States accounts for over a quarter of the world's economic activity; it is the world's largest trader and international investor; it is the leader in technological and managerial innovation; and in recent years its culture has spread farther and faster than that of any other nation. The United States has been the strongest proponent of economic systems based on the rule of law. At the heart of this philosophy is the sound governance of national economies and companies—governance based on transparent and accurate financial accounting. The Enron disaster and all that followed it undermined much of what America claimed it stood for. The series of scandals also gave opponents of U.S.-style capitalism stronger arguments against the free-market policies and the regulatory prescriptions that the United States has advocated.

It is difficult to overestimate how much an erosion of support for American ideas would affect further globalization. Between 1945 and 1989, the entire free world took its economic policy cues from Wall Street and Washington. After the Soviet Union collapsed, virtually every country jumped aboard the same train. In China and India, home to more than 30 percent of the world's population, government officials have adopted many elements of the American model of capitalism. Stock market officials from Turkey and Brazil want to know how the New York Stock Exchange and the NASDAQ work. Corporate governance in Deutsche Bank AG or in Toyota Motor Corporation is looking more and more like that of Citigroup or General Motors. The American economic philosophy has been the driving force of the world economy, and if it is discredited by disgraceful corporate behavior—the risk of which is real—the global economy could be in considerable disarray. Paul Volcker said it well in congressional testimony:

> We have been critical of the relative weakness of accounting and auditing standards in many other countries, arguing that those weaknesses have contributed to the volatility, inefficiency and breakdown of the financial systems. How ironic that, at this point in economic history

when the performance of the American economy and financial markets has been so seemingly successful, we are faced with such doubts and questions about a system of accounting and auditing in which we have taken so much pride, threatening the credibility and confidence essential to well-functioning markets. . . . The implications extend far beyond the shores of the United States.[1]

The combined effect of the war on terrorism and the growing mistrust in the integrity of financial markets and corporations comes at a delicate time in the world economy. It is difficult to see where the locomotive force for economic growth will come from. Even a recovery in the United States is unlikely to duplicate the strength it had in the latter half of the 1990s. Japan could be in relative stagnation for years to come, making the world's second largest economy a net drain. The European Union is projected to grow only modestly. Meanwhile, there is little sign of any industrial sector becoming a strong leading edge for investment.

Beyond these sobering conditions, there is a good chance that the campaign against terrorism and the upheaval in corporate America's governance will fall particularly hard on developing nations. Foreign direct investment has been slowing, as companies are besieged about charges of malfeasance at home and worried about corporate governance issues abroad. Tourism, the lifeblood of so many third-world nations, has been badly hurt by travelers' concerns about security. As will be explained, the curtailing of immigration flows in response to September 11 and other fears is also a body blow to emerging markets that depend heavily on remittances.

Finally, there are the precarious conditions in global financial markets themselves. For all the talk of a stock market slump, today's price-earnings ratios in the United States are still twice the historical averages. For all the talk about a weaker dollar, the U.S. currency is still overvalued by any technical analysis. So, considerable global economic risks are in the background.

There are three reasons why CEOs need to work with governments to create the right balance of public and private interests in the global economy. First, because international companies are held together by intricate global webs of money, people, and supplies, any disruption of globalization will be a severe blow to their fortunes. In this hypercompetitive world, in which pricing margins are under severe pressure, the establishment of large-scale operations has become crucial. Research costs have soared and thus need to be spread over a worldwide base of business. Since customers' needs and tastes vary around the world, companies must be located close to their markets. Companies must also be able to tap into local sources of finance and have a significant local presence in order to hire the most talented people. Their operations depend on hundreds of suppliers and many more subcontractors in every corner of the globe, all of which must be exquisitely coordinated. As we saw after September 11, this web of relationships is extremely vulnerable. In interviews with business leaders here and abroad, I have heard over and over that their number one fear about the future is that the trend of globalization would be disrupted.

The fortunes of global companies also depend on the health of the societies in which they work. Sustaining globalization means sustaining trade. And trade—while not sufficient in itself—is a critical ingredient in the growth and vitality of virtually any nation today. Surveying the last century, Daniel Yergin, author of *The Commanding Heights: The Battle between Government and the Marketplace That Is Remaking the Modern World*, observed that history shows that open economies that engage in trade have the best chance to grow and prosper.[2] His views are supported by numerous studies by The World Bank and other institutions. If trade patterns were to slow or even reverse, as they did at the end of the last great age of globalization (1870–1914), not only would companies' operations be disrupted, but their markets and the societies in which they operate would suffer.

Second, governments need help. Symbolic of the shortcomings of public-sector efforts is the institution once called the Group of Seven (G7) and now known as the G8, because of the recent addition of Russia. The high-water mark of the group's efforts is its annual summit meeting. When the G7 was founded in 1975—in the face of a global energy crisis, soaring inflation, and growing unemployment—it represented a major leap forward in managing globalization. But over the years, the group's annual meetings have become little more than media extravaganzas. Most of the official communiqués are written well in advance, and the meetings are taken up with little more than brokering key sentences and phrases. Ultimately these reports are written in bureaucratic language indecipherable by ordinary citizens. To the extent that they contain new initiatives, few outside the inner circles of individual governments have any idea whether the proposed programs were ever followed up or what their impact has been.

The ineffectiveness of the G8 reflects a fundamental limitation of the role of governments in the world economy. The key issue is the relative power of markets versus regulators. Markets have grown in size and complexity and have spread well beyond national boundaries. More than $1.5 trillion of foreign-exchange transactions take place every day. The trading in complex derivatives across borders amounts to many multiples of that. In the early 1980s, government-backed foreign aid used to be at least four times the amount of private capital flows to the developing world, but by 2002 it's just the opposite: Private investment is about six times greater than foreign aid from governments. Meanwhile, governments have been under chronic pressure to shrink their scope of activity. Much of their best talent—or the talent that might once have entered the public service—is moving to the private sector. There, the professional opportunities and compensation are much greater and a person has far less chance of being embroiled in career-breaking political controversies. In an era in which organizations need sophisticated expertise to understand how global finance and trade operate, governments are at a big disadvantage in their efforts to monitor what is going on, let alone regulate it. Then, too, each government has a responsibility to its own citizens, not to anyone else; governments' mind-set is domestic, not international. With precious few tools to deal with powerful global markets, governments must coordinate policies with other governments and create, support, and work through international institutions. Though important to do, these activities are difficult to do effectively and consistently.

A third reason why we need a stronger business voice to help manage the global economy is that enlightened executives can help balance the opposing forces of freedom and order. Most successful global business leaders are vigorous proponents of open economies. Their organizations thrive when barriers to commerce are removed and when the ingenuity of their employees is free to flower. On the other hand, most global CEOs are not ideologues, but are the ultimate pragmatists. They require a certain level of predictability, and they want a public-policy framework that insures fair competition and enforces the rules. They want effective governments—governments capable of setting rules and enforcing them in a transparent and fair way. Global CEOs know that business and anarchy don't mix. The very strength of this central conviction makes them good partners for governments in managing the global economy.

AGENDA ITEM: BUSINESS LEADERS SHOULD WORK TO KEEP THE WORLD ECONOMY OPEN IN THE FACE OF STRONG HEAD WINDS

One critical task for CEOs is to survey all the measures that have been put in place—or are contemplated—to pursue the war on terrorism. The executives would then be in a better position to speak to the government in constructive ways about the balance between regulation and open markets.

Under the assumption that we have not seen the last of terrorist attacks in the United States and abroad, we can reasonably assume that governments' role in the global arena will continue to intensify. A good example is the U.S.-led global effort to close down the channels that terrorists use to finance their operations. In the period of just a few weeks after September 11, the U.S. Congress passed legislation tightening surveillance on all financial transactions in the U.S. banking system and closing down the operations of groups suspected of terrorist activities or of supporting them. The Departments of Treasury and Justice put pressure on banks and securities companies to engage in unprecedented information sharing, allowing law enforcement agencies to check on a daily basis the individuals and organizations on their lists of terrorists against the financial firms' databases. Washington also pressed the United Nations, the International Monetary Fund, and the Organization for Economic Cooperation and Development to help identify suspicious financial flows. The twenty-nine-member Financial Action Task Force, an ad-hoc group of major governments, was urged to block all channels that could be supportive to terrorists in their countries. The United States and the European Union established lists of terrorist organizations, publicized them globally, and pressured other governments to close down any accounts that belonged to them. Taken together, these activities forced governments to levy sanctions, freeze assets, blacklist recalcitrant governments, demand information from depositors and customers, and scrutinize trusts, foundations, charities, and partnerships.

This effort to get control over potentially criminal financial transactions breaks new ground. In the past, financial investigations occurred *in response* to an event. After a crime was committed, an investigation would then take place to trace the flow of money related to it. Now there is an effort to head off transactions *in advance* of a criminal act. Banks were once urged to know where their deposits were *coming from*—who or what the source of the money was. Now banks are being held responsible for knowing who or what is *receiving* these funds and what the party plans to do with the money. In the past, commercial banks were the principal targets of surveillance and investigation, because in taking deposits and making loans, they knew precisely who their customers were. But the scope of financial regulation is widening now, reaching to brokerage firms, investment funds, and mortgage lenders. In April 2002, the U.S. Treasury issued a new legal requirement that virtually all financial intermediaries—including real estate agents, credit card companies, wire transfer companies like Western Union, and check-cashing outlets—must report any financial transaction greater than five thousand dollars, and even smaller amounts if it appears that the customer is intentionally trying to avoid detection. The new rules mandated that financial companies appoint chief compliance officers and establish training programs to heighten employees' knowledge of the new rules.

The magnitude of this new financial regulatory effort is all the more remarkable because it has been acknowledged that terrorists rely on relatively little financing to accomplish their aims. Hence, unlike the hunt for money related to illegal trade in narcotics, in which large amounts of funds are transferred around the world, the search for terrorists' funds is far more labor-intensive and requires a much deeper government probe into the daily operations of monetary flows. After its exhaustive efforts for seven months after the terrorist attacks, the United States had identified only $104 million belonging to alleged terrorists. In a world whose gross domestic product is $40 trillion, and in which the United States alone borrows more than $1 billion per day from abroad, this $104 million isn't even a rounding error.

One of the reasons why so little money has been sequestered is that terrorists have probably moved into commodity trading, drug trafficking, and other criminal activity.[3] This trend could produce a widening of governments' efforts—understandable, to be sure, but raising the question, Where is it all leading?

Actions that trace money flows spill over into other sensitive arenas, too. In February 2002, the United States encouraged several Middle Eastern and Asian countries to establish their own independent intelligence units in order to trace and monitor the flows of funds in and out of the country on a retail basis—that is, lender by lender, investor by investor. At a meeting of G7 finance ministers two months later, the Bush administration turned up the pressure, issuing thinly veiled threats of penalties for those governments that fail to move decisively. Though understandable in the context of antiterrorism, increased government involvement in countries' financial business expands governments' intrusion into their nations' economies in several ways. It could impede economic liberalization and could create a level of societal intrusion that undercuts the prospects for more open political systems.[4]

How can we evaluate all this in the context of an open global economy? In a heightened state of national security, when survival is seen to be in the balance and financing is a key element in the enemy's ability to operate, a government must take all the measures that might impede terrorists. But the extent of government activity in finance raises questions about how far regulation will go and whether there are adequate countervailing forces to raise the necessary alarms if intervention has gone too far, is constricting too much legitimate economic activity, or simply constitutes unnecessary burdens on commerce. With today's computer capabilities, governments will have so much information about individuals and organizations—not just terrorists or those suspected of harboring them, but all of us—that the potential for misuse will rise exponentially. A government might inadvertently and publicly disclose information about someone's private but legitimate financial dealings. Intentional misuse of that information by a nefarious government or subversive elements within it is not difficult to imagine, either.

The management of immigration is another arena in which concerted controls, information gathering by governments, and collaboration across borders could get out of hand. Since September 11, 2001, the United States has become more concerned about immigration. There are, for example, powerful pressures to tighten visa requirements. Under the April 2002 presidential directive entitled "Combating Terrorism through Immigration Policy," the Bush administration was not only considering subjecting incoming students to more rigorous background checks but also restricting what they can study when they arrive in the United States. At a minimum, foreign students will be more carefully monitored by the Justice Department and university administrators, and the system that is being designed for that purpose could easily become the model for tightening surveillance of other groups of foreign visitors. Beyond students, tourist visas were being shortened from six months to thirty days, business visas from twelve to six months.

The establishment of a Department of Homeland Security will add another powerful player to U.S. immigration policy—and probably not one that views immigration as a positive phenomenon. If the new agency includes the Immigration and

Naturalization Service, as well as the State Department visa-granting section—as some early blueprints indicated it would—then it would be understandable, but unfortunate, if a strong bureaucratic bias emerged to keep people out, as opposed to showing an understanding of how critical the influx of immigrants and refugees has been to American society.

In Europe, there are political moves to tighten restrictions, a policy intertwined not only with terrorism but with growing concern for law and order and with the rise of nationalism. "The ultranationalist, xenophobic right is manifestly on the rise, and not just in France," wrote European analyst Tony Judt in the *New York Times* in April 2002.[5] He cited Austria, Switzerland, Holland, and Denmark as part of the trend. Indeed, in the interest of identifying and tracking down terrorists, immigration officials the world over are now trying to gather more information on who is entering and leaving their countries. They are working closely with intelligence and law-enforcement agencies within their countries and with those of other nations. They will be using advanced technologies for recognizing people and amassing information on them.

One important part of the new concerns about immigration involves some 35 million people who are fleeing war or political persecution around the world. Such refugees who wish to come to the United States are facing investigations far more intensive than ever before. There are more interrogations, a deeper examination of personal histories, more restrictions on travel arrangements, more profiling by country and ethnic background. Governments worldwide are allowing fewer refugees to enter their borders. In the United States, the quota had already been declining since the mid-1980s—70,000 in 2001 compared with 200,000 fifteen years earlier—but since September 11, resettlement has come to a near halt. In Australia, Denmark, and elsewhere, severe new restrictions are also being implemented.[6]

Even normal travel is subject to new arrangements. In early February 2002, the U.S. government and several airlines announced that they would be coordinating their databases with those of other governments and carriers in order to create in-depth profiles of passengers and to gather information on how they bought their tickets, where else they had traveled, and their spending habits.[7] With such a vast, interconnected database, it will be as though all your credit and debit cards and all significant financial transactions were linked in one database that any airline ticket clerk could call up. Given that terrorism is global, one of the hallmarks of the era is that the actions taken in just one country are not sufficient for protection; hence we are on the verge of global production and sharing of such extensive profiling. As with tracing the flow of money, the issue isn't whether such information is necessary, because the terrorist threat leaves us little choice. But business leaders and public officials ought to be asking how we can insure that the movement of people across borders for legitimate purposes isn't constricted and how the unprecedented amount of personal data that governments intend to gather now is not misused.

In the end, there are enormous costs to cutting back on the movement of people around the world. It should go without saying—but perhaps it should be said anyway—that the United States would not exist in any recognizable form with the vitality, the productivity, the socio-economic and political framework that has been forged, if we were not a nation of immigrants. From Wall Street to Silicon Valley, from Miami to Milwaukee, the infusion of energy and talent from abroad has been pivotal. Looking ahead, an aging Europe's future is in more immigration, too. There is no other solution if the EU is to be a vibrant set of nations and not a lethargic retirement home. So what is happening now on the immigration front is deeply antithetical to the region from Portugal to the Baltics. And no one will suffer more than the developing nations who last year received more than $100 billion in remittances from their citizens abroad. In Mexico, such remittances are the third largest source of foreign exchange after oil and tourism. In Turkey, these flows are four times larger than those from foreign direct investment.[8]

A third area worthy of CEO concern and monitoring is the added costs of more intense inspection of cargo at the borders. About 90 percent of all trade moves by sea, most of it in containers, and most of it not scrutinized by customs officials. As part of a plan to enhance security at ports and during the transport of containers to their ultimate destinations, governments are moving toward an international system of screening. This will require techno-logical innovation—such as X-ray machines and transponders in terminals—as well as the establishment of special security zones in port areas and extensive international coordination. There are other ideas afloat, too, all understandable in the context of the war, but also potentially expensive and disruptive. For example, the United States could extend border controls to the factory or warehouse where the container is first filled.[9] The products of suppliers who failed to comply could be denied entry into the United States. These new techniques will raise the cost of shipping, and business will pay for it in many ways—handling fees, added risk insurance, delays in delivery. In addition, as the United States seeks to transfer to foreign ports the responsibility for inspections, it will shy away from all but the biggest and most sophisticated ones, those that can afford modern detection equipment. The upshot could well be that the ports of develop-ing countries find their trade drying up—another hammer blow to their economic prospects.

The potential for rising costs for importing food could be

another problem. Both houses of Congress have passed a bill that would increase inspections of incoming agricultural products. It would require food manufacturers and processors to register with the government and authorize the Food and Drug Administration to detain food products without a court order. In the spring of 2002, the National Food Processing Association, not surprisingly, was opposing what, according to the *New York Times,* would be "the most significant expansion of federal authority over the food industry in six decades."[10] Among the concerns of companies like Kraft Foods, H. J. Heinz, and ConAgra Foods was the possibility that in doing their inspections, federal agents would gain access to consumer complaint files and trade secrets, all of which would be subsequently released to the public via the Freedom of Information Act.

Business leaders and government officials need to watch the further expansion of government into finance, immigration, cargo inspection, and the like, because of costs and other barriers to commerce that could inadvertently be protectionist in their impact. But the overall concern of CEOs should be that government power gained in one arena is easily extended to another. Once the precedent is set, once bureaucracies are established, once there is a mind-set that national security encompasses everything, how far are we from overbearing regulation in many more areas—and how far are we from a serious undermining of free-market economies? It's a politically tricky and very delicate balance for society to make these days. But it's a balance on which the top business executives need to express their views—because more than any other group, they have the most direct interest in making an effective case for the most open possible global economic system.

AGENDA ITEM: BUSINESS LEADERS
SHOULD REDOUBLE EFFORTS TO
LIBERALIZE GLOBAL TRADE

CEOs should be pressing governments to keep a keen eye on opening new avenues for trade, investment, and the movement of people. It is more important than ever that the global business community get behind the upcoming negotiations, under the auspices of the World Trade Organization (WTO) in Geneva, to lower barriers to world trade. Mounting this effort could be more difficult than it sounds. It certainly won't be helped by the lessening of both the volume and the value of world trade these past two years.

The last round of global trade negotiations, which ended in 1993, took more than seven years to complete. For whatever reasons—the lack of understanding of what really was at stake, the recession of the early 1990s, competing domestic priorities—multinational business leaders did little to push the negotiations forward. It is not hard to envision a repeat of this attitude of neglect. In fact, it appears to already be happening, as so much attention has shifted from global negotiations to bilateral trade disputes between the United States and Europe. It is very possible, moreover, that another factor has intruded since the last set of global trade negotiations—the increasingly short-term focus of CEOs. Think of it this way: If you were being held to quarterly results and your job was constantly on the line if you failed to perform, and in any event your job tenure was unlikely to be more than five to six years—the CEO average—how much attention would you pay to trade negotiations that would pay off a decade from now? Nevertheless, for the United States as a nation, it would be dangerous if CEOs underestimated the shifting popular tide against major trade liberalization today. How trade policy is made, how it's implemented, what its relationship

should be to labor practices and environmental protection—
these have become highly contentious political issues in Washington. Absent serious attention, corporate America could easily
find itself in an environment with stalled momentum for trade
liberalization. Given the outsized role of the United States in
the world economy, this could cause the onset of protectionism
on a global scale.

A good example of the beginnings of protectionism is the decision by President Bush in March 2002 to place import restrictions on steel products. Even his own chief trade negotiator,
Robert Zoellick, admitted that the major reason for imposing
this protection was to appease certain domestic pressures. The
American steel industry has been in decline for years; protection
might buy some time, but it will not revive companies now inca-
pable of competing globally. In past years, at least some government officials and businesspeople would have said, "We need a
strong steel industry for national security." This time there was
hardly an attempt to use that argument.

In reaction to the administration's decision, a chorus of
complaints came from American users of steel, who now faced
higher prices for supplies. But such hand-wringing was nothing
compared to the outrage in Europe and elsewhere. The European Union, Japan, and other nations said they planned to sue
the United States in the WTO. The international agitation
caused by American protectionism is now bound to spill over
into other arenas of trade. It has become all too legitimate to
ask: How credible is America's professed commitment to more
open markets?

Another big trade problem caused by U.S. policy is in agriculture. Reversing 1996 legislation that sought to reduce government aid to farmers, both houses of Congress, in the spring of
2002, passed a farm bill that raises agricultural subsidies by over
80 percent over the next ten years, with no provision for phasing

out the supports. The new bill increases subsidies for soybeans, wheat, and corn, and establishes new subsidies for peanuts, lentils, and dairy farms. The bill has the effect of encouraging the farmers to grow crops in excess of market demands, thereby causing oversupply and depressing prices around the world. This policy is directly contrary to everything that Washington has professed to stand for in international trade policy. "America's commitment to freer trade looks laughable," said the *Economist*.[11]

American chief executives made a big mistake in not trying to head off the steel decision and in being so quiet on the issue of agricultural subsidies. The problem is broader, however. Many top CEOs are so preoccupied with meeting competitive threats that they believe they have neither the time nor the inclination to get involved in high-level trade policy. Thinking that continued globalization is inevitable anyway, some executives are content to leave the negotiations to governments. But given the recent expansion of governmental intervention in global commerce, business leaders must make a commensurate effort to knock down barriers to trade and investment. The business world cannot gamble that globalization will continue out of momentum or someone else's hard work.

To this end, global CEOs ought to be articulating and lobbying for a far-reaching agenda for trade liberalization. They should be pressing governments to move ahead with the negotiations launched in November 2001 at Doha, Qatar. They should be energizing the business community and helping to educate the public as to why people should support expanded trade. By scanning the entire range of global transactions, CEOs could find new ways to liberalize government regulations that impede free flows of goods, services, ideas, and people. Obviously this is different from what governments preoccupied with national security are doing. But we need the countervailing force of ideas and action from the private sector.

AGENDA ITEM: CEOS SHOULD SUPPORT
HIGHER LEVELS OF INVESTMENT IN GLOBAL
RULES AND INSTITUTIONS

Business leaders should also work to strengthen the framework for the world economy—the rules and institutions within which markets operate. The leaders have a stake in a marketplace based on the rule of law and on clear and enforceable rules that balance freedom and order. Where the right laws do not exist, or when different legal systems clash, businesses incur higher costs and the world economy becomes inefficient.

CEOs ought to be acknowledging that sovereignty is waning and that more authority has to devolve to global institutions. This is a politically radical stance, to be sure, but much of the national control that nations once had over their economic and commercial affairs has clearly been lost forever. Real influence can and should be wielded in international forums. For this reason, the United States must take international governance much more seriously. It should invest in multilateral institutions, insuring that they have good people and strong charters, operate with transparent due process, and are held accountable for results. This *is* the new order—or at least it should be, if the objective is to expand global commerce in a sustainable way. More than most other groups, CEOs ought to understand that a global economy cannot be overseen by national governments trying to apply their varying policies and politics and that one of the great challenges of this new century is to build a truly global foundation for a global economy.

Business leaders should give more of their attention to a number of areas. The International Monetary Fund, the WTO, and The World Bank all require business support and advice. Several international efforts to develop new rules are also important. Business and the world economy would benefit by more coordinated arrangements between countries for the regulation of mergers and acquisitions. Today more than sixty different antitrust regimes exist, which raises the business and governmental cost of assessing and implementing global corporate combinations. There is also a need for more formal and systematic arrangements for sovereign debt defaults; the current system is chaotic and costly to banks and governments alike. The world needs better ways to insure food safety; there is no international equivalent of the U.S. Food and Drug Administration. The regime for intellectual property rights in the Internet age needs to be strengthened. The world's reliance on the Internet and similar data-sharing technology also requires a framework for privacy laws governing the use of business data and preventing the rise of contradictory laws in different countries. The importance of international standards for accounting has been discussed in chapter 5. In these and other areas, the requirement is to balance sound regulation with open markets—to establish a pattern of promarket regulation. And that will only happen with enlightened participation on the part of business leaders, especially given the counterpressure of government regulation unleashed after September 11, 2001.

There is a great risk that amid the preoccupation with the war against terrorism and the Enron-Andersen debacle, Washington and corporate America will lose sight of the reality that the most powerful force acting on the nation—and the world—is globalization. It is easy to take for granted that the opening of the world economy will continue, and that the expansion of trade and foreign investment is an irrevocable trend. Such assumptions would be a grave mistake. Maintaining an open world economy will require much work on the part of governments and corporate leaders, working with nongovernmental organizations as well. This is all the more true given the powerful centrifugal forces unleashed by recent events.

CHAPTER 8

REDUCING GLOBAL POVERTY

O NE PROBLEM at the nexus of an open world economy and national security is global poverty. A 2001 United Nations report, echoing what so many other analyses have concluded, described some of the conditions that exist. Approximately 20 percent of the world's population still lives on less than one dollar per day, and half live below two dollars per day. One-quarter is still illiterate. In the poorest countries, home to 2.5 billion people, infant mortality is fifteen times the rate in rich countries.[1] "The poverty challenge is getting bigger, and harder," said The World Bank president, James D. Wolfensohn. "In 25 years, global population will go up by 2 billion people, 98 percent of whom will be in poor and developing countries. There will be wider inequalities, between countries and within countries."[2]

Since September 11, 2001, poverty has appeared more prominently on the international agenda than it has in several decades. But this heightened attention is also counterbalanced by a sense of cynicism—a conviction that the problems are of such overwhelming magnitude and social complexity that any large-scale approach is bound to fail. In its first year, this sort of "development fatigue" gripped the Bush administration, which still seems to have an inclination to dwell on military actions abroad and leave the financing of development to the Europeans and

Japanese. Treasury Secretary Paul O'Neill has been particularly skeptical: "Over the last fifty years, the developed world has spent trillions in the name of aid. And I would submit we have precious little to show for it."[3]

In mid-2000, a group of world leaders, under the auspices of the U.N., reached consensus on a number of targets to improve the lives of people around the world living in abject poverty. At the Millennium Summit, the leaders agreed to cut extreme poverty in half within fifteen years, by tackling some of its worst symptoms and its most obstinate causes. Some of the specific targets included the following: to reduce the number of people living on less than a dollar a day; to eliminate gender disparity at all levels of education; to reduce child mortality rates by two-thirds; to decrease maternal mortality by three-quarters; to substantially roll back HIV/AIDS, malaria, and other diseases; and to halve the number of people without access to safe water.[4] To meet these objectives, the governments of poor countries will need to reorient their policies to benefit their poorest citizens, and the richer nations will have to open their markets and their wallets. At the beginning of 2002, U.N. Secretary-General Kofi Annan believed the momentum was already slipping: "Prevailing approaches to development remain fragmented and piecemeal," he said. "Funding is woefully inadequate; and production and consumption patterns continue to overburden the world's natural life-support systems."[5]

There are many reasons why this situation is a danger to the global economy and requires high-level attention. Aside from the obvious moral imperative to insure that those in desperate need have a way out of their misery, poverty bears a high economic cost: people who are far less productive, because they are uneducated or sick; markets that are less vibrant, because there is no purchasing power; governmental allocation of scarce financial resources to subsidize the poor, when those resources might have gone to investment that would lead to expanded growth for everyone. The future holds significant prospects for trade, investment, sales, and the acquisition of talent in areas that are now poor, but need not remain so, say C. K. Prahalad and Stuart L. Hart: "The lackluster nature of most [multinational corporations'] emerging market strategies over the past decade does not change the magnitude of the opportunity. The real source of market promise is not the wealthy few in the developing world, or even the emerging middle-income consumers: It is the billions of *aspiring poor* who are joining the market economy for the first time."[6]

There is also a security dimension to poverty. Although we shouldn't strain to make the direct connection between the men who attacked the World Trade Center and the Pentagon and the despair that exists in so many countries, terrorists are more likely to have their roots in, and gain popular support from, populations that see the future as hopeless. Poverty fosters weak governments and civil wars and creates opportunities for terrorists to operate with relative impunity. In addition, as in the case of the September 11 attackers, sometimes people who leave these poverty-stricken societies to be educated abroad carry the scars of their homeland with them. Their rage reflects the wide gap between the political and economic culture they left and the new one that they cannot join or even get accustomed to.

For all these reasons there must be a global coalition against poverty, just as there is one against terrorism. And the participants ought to be not just governments but an alliance of multinational corporations, international institutions, and nongovernmental organizations (NGOs).

Business leaders should press their governments to make the reduction of poverty a higher priority, and they ought to get more involved on the ground in countries where they have operations. CEOs are, by and large, optimists. They start with the idea that big challenges can be overcome. Being realists also, they understand that rhetorical goals must be matched by specific targets, measurable results, and personal accountability. Were they to bring these qualities to the awesome challenge in the developing world, that alone would be an invaluable contribution.

AGENDA ITEM: CEOS SHOULD PRESS FOR TRADE POLICIES THAT BENEFIT POOR COUNTRIES

I have already underscored the role that business leaders should play to encourage trade liberalization in general. But it will take an extra effort, and one requiring even more political capital, to press governments to pursue policies for trade liberalization aimed specifically at giving poor countries better access to the markets of wealthy nations. In the past, trade has always been driven by the needs of the industrialized world, but if economic progress is to spread around the globe, governments and businesses must take more account of the requirements of poor countries. This will mean going against the political grain in the United States and other advanced industrial nations. "The steps which industrial economies will need to make if they are serious about helping the world's poorest to develop their economies have barely begun to register with [their] political leaders," said *The Economist.*[7]

The magazine is right. According to The World Bank, the tariffs that high-income countries impose on products from developing countries are four times those collected from rich countries. The countries of the developed world also spend about $1 billion per day to subsidize their own agricultural production of products that poor countries export; that's about six times the amount spent on all development assistance combined. Also, industrial economies have instituted special means to protect sensitive industries such as steel and textiles—industries in which the developing nations have natural advantages. In other words, the rich nations are sending capital to the third world to develop their industries, but blocking the international markets for the products that could be sold. Lacking overseas markets, these poorer countries cannot attract adequate investment. It's a vicious downward cycle.[8]

Business leaders can spotlight these inequities and lobby their governments to address them in the upcoming trade negotiations. They also need to press governments not to take away with one hand what they extend with another. In the 1980s, the United States gave special trade concessions to the countries of the Caribbean basin. As the price for getting the House of Representatives to give President Bush new trade negotiating authority in 2001, these benefits were quietly subject to new legislative reviews that weakened them considerably. In 2000, Washington passed legislation opening U.S. markets to textiles and other products of poor African countries. It is important that these remain on the books and not be chipped away in the labyrinth of U.S. domestic politics. Business leaders willing to promote real trade liberalization for poor nations will also have to rein in many of their colleagues who are the biggest proponents of protectionism—in industries such as steel, dairy, and textiles. Fighting this tide of protectionism will be politically difficult, but standing up against popular sentiment is exactly what global leadership entails.

AGENDA ITEM: CEOS SHOULD PRESS FOR INCREASES IN FOREIGN ASSISTANCE

The world needs a powerful set of voices outside the U.S. government advocating higher levels of aid and more effective use of the funds. Precisely what is needed can only be estimated in orders of magnitude. A U.N. commission, cochaired by former Mexican president Ernesto Zedillo, and including former U.S. Treasury Secretary Robert Rubin, has indicated that at least an incremental $50 billion per year is required to substantially reduce poverty—twice as much as the aid flowing today.[9] Yet the trend is in the opposite direction: Total aid in 2002 adjusted for inflation was about 10 percent lower than it was a decade before then.[10]

CEOs should press the Congress and the Bush administration to increase the levels of America's foreign aid, and they also need to make the case with the public. The performance of the U.S. government has been dismal by any standard. The United States provides 0.1 percent of its GDP in foreign aid, the lowest percentage of any major industrial country and less than a third of European levels. Over the last decade, American foreign aid has declined by over 30 percent, when inflation is stripped out. There is room to argue about how the aid ought to be used, how to link it to policies in recipient countries, and how to measure its impact—and CEOs can bring a lot to this debate. But if America doesn't step up its performance, other countries won't either.

Foreign aid from the United States and other countries should also include more assistance for debt relief for the poorest nations, in return for their own governments' pursuit of sound policies. A major international initiative on debt relief is under way and deserves the support of the United States, not only to implement what is on the table now, but to expand the scope of the plan. Financial help is also needed for the budgets of the U.N.'s specialized agencies. Increased support for the World Health Organization and for those agencies that oversee aid for children, food production in poor countries, refugees services, and the reconstruction of states recovering from civil wars is critical. The budgets of institutions like the World Trade Organization must also provide for essential technical assistance to developing countries, whose officials lack the expertise to negotiate international economic arrangements that will give them a chance to take advantage of what globalization can offer them. For instance, a typical developing country spends $250 million per year just to implement three of the dozens of agreements that constitute membership in the WTO: agreements on customs valuation, intellectual property rights, and technical standards. That's more than the average country's entire annual budget for roads, communications, and other development projects.[11]

In the spring of 2002, the politics of foreign aid began to change in Washington, although it was not clear by how much. At a global conference on financing for development, held in Monterrey, Mexico, in mid-March 2002, President Bush announced that the United States would increase its annual development aid budget by 50 percent by 2006. Although the funds would be dispensed only after Washington was satisfied that the recipients had followed a host of sound policies, the Bush administration's U-turn generally pleased the international community. Still, what America didn't like about foreign aid was clearer than what it did. "For decades, success of development aid was measured only in resources spent, and not in results achieved," said President Bush. "Pouring money into a status quo does little to help the poor."[12] Three months later, the Bush administration proposed doubling the amount of money it spends on education in Africa and substantially increasing funding for dealing with HIV/AIDS on the continent.

The business community needs now to press Washington to keep up the new momentum. The increases in American aid, while welcome if they in fact materialize, still fall far short of what is necessary. Also, virtually no part of the new plan can be implemented without congressional support, and business pressure on Capitol Hill will be a critical element in getting any new approach off the ground.

Foreign aid to help the poor has been unpopular in the United States ever since the Marshall Plan was completed. Even if and when the new U.S. approach announced by President

Bush is combined with new aid pledges from Europe and elsewhere, the total aid would constitute less than 20 percent of the goals supported by the U.N. Given the political realities and the problems that will ensue if poverty continues to spread and deepen, a more radical approach ought to be considered: a global tax on trade, or on carbon emissions, or on sales of military equipment. Most governments and business executives consider such ideas heretical. But if you know that the course you are on is bound to fail—if the problems grow faster than the remedies you have been trying—is it so crazy to think about approaches of a different order of magnitude? In a system of global taxation of some kind, revenues would be funneled into one or more trust funds that would be available, under precise guidelines, for investments in poor countries. Choosing who would manage those funds would be a crucial decision, of course. Many other fundamentals of any plan—the rate of the tax, the collection procedures, the allocation mechanism, etc.—would have to be worked out. However, if business leaders took a serious interest in such plans and participated in thinking them through, it would help to diffuse the objections that the plans are socialist schemes. After all, there are no advanced societies in which taxes do not help fund pressing social investments.

AGENDA ITEM: BUSINESS LEADERS SHOULD HELP EASE THE CRISIS IN GLOBAL HEALTH

No single project would pay more dividends to poor people and poor countries than a revitalized and larger-scale approach to combating disease in the third world. Better health is a worthy end in itself, but it is also a key to development. The policy agenda is superbly set out in a report released in December 2001 by the World Health Organization's Commission on Macroeconomics and Health, *Macroeconomics and Health: Investing in Health for Economic Development*. The report identified the communicable diseases that exist in developing countries, the human and economic toll they take, and the importance of changing internal policies of third-world governments and significantly increasing financial assistance from the wealthy nations. The main causes of avoidable deaths in the low-income countries are HIV/AIDS, malaria, tuberculosis, childhood infectious diseases, and poor maternal and child health. The commission advocates an interlocking joint effort by rich and poor nations.[13]

CEOs could play a number of roles in this critical project. Indeed, several prominent companies have already laid out an agenda for themselves and their corporate colleagues. They include Alcoa, The Coca-Cola Company, DaimlerChrysler, Exxon-Mobil, Pfizer, Inc., Nestlé S.A., and Heineken N.V., all of which have come together under the auspices of the Global Health Initiative, organized by the World Economic Forum in Geneva. Among their recommendations were that companies should continuously monitor and treat the impact of infectious diseases on their workforces; that they ought to undertake long-term cost-benefit and effectiveness evaluations of intervention programs and share their findings with host governments and nongovernmental organizations (NGOs); that they should share their information with their suppliers and distributors; and that they should participate in new global funds being established, such as the Global Fund to Fight AIDS, TB, and Malaria. The Commission on Macroeconomics and Health also implores companies to become more involved in research and development into specific tropical diseases that are concentrated in poor countries, and it asks pharmaceutical firms in particular to help developing nations obtain vaccines and other medicines at affordable costs. All these measures are worthy of increased CEO attention.

AGENDA ITEM: CEOS SHOULD
CONTRIBUTE TO THE EVOLUTION
OF DEVELOPMENT STRATEGY

There is great ferment in the field of development theory, where many big questions are hotly debated: What should be the balance between investing in essential physical infrastructure—such as telecommunications and energy generation—and investing in social programs, like education and health? To what extent should foreign assistance be made conditional on internal government reform, and how much is necessary as a precondition to that reform? What are the best ways to build local institutions to lift people out of poverty? There are no perfect answers, but at least The World Bank, the International Money Fund, the WTO, many NGOs, and the governments of developing nations themselves are searching for answers. If the corporate world is being asked to participate in the attack on global poverty—as it is—then it should be part of this examination.

Another way for business leaders to be engaged is to fund joint business-government research in new development theories. They could take a close look at the work of the Peruvian economist Hernando de Soto, whose book, *The Mystery of Capital: Why Capitalism Triumphs in the West and Fails Everywhere Else,* explains that by passing laws to make it easier for poor people to gain title to their homes and small businesses, a tidal wave of potential credit will ensue, leading to an expanded entrepreneurial culture. "It is not enough to appeal to the stomachs of the poor," de Soto writes, reflecting on September 11. "One must appeal to their aspirations. This is, in a way, what the terrorists do. But their path leads only to destruction. Any campaign that does not drive a political and economic wedge between terrorists and the poor is likely to be short-lived."[14]

Business leaders could mount their own creative development efforts. Take the case of a Cisco Systems program called Net.Aid, an idea generated by CEO John Chambers and a group of company and outside professionals. Cisco teamed up with the United Nations Development Program (UNDP) to use the Internet to combat poverty. Cisco takes responsibility for creating and maintaining an elaborate Web site (netaid.org) that allows people to better understand the nature of poverty and get personally involved in a specific program by matching their own capabilities to specific needs in poor countries. On the Web site, a donor can identify a specific challenge in the third world—such as hunger, medicine, or education. He or she can contribute funds and then track the impact of the commitment. The UNDP is the on-the-ground agent in more than a hundred countries. This is an experiment, to be sure, but Chambers's combination of corporations, public entities, and information technology is innovative.

Another example is the Bill & Melinda Gates Foundation. Virtually no one else has the resources of Microsoft's Bill Gates, but many multinational companies run major foundations. For an example of imaginative and highly disciplined development assistance, the companies should take a hard look at what the Bill & Melinda Gates Foundation is doing to fight disease in poor countries. The program is a highly results-oriented undertaking in which Gates has applied business principles to global health. Governments of recipient countries have to increase their own spending on health in order to get assistance. Nor will assistance flow unless there is evidence that it will be a catalyst for a self-sustaining program. The foundation audits the performance of grant recipients. "[Gates] has helped create a whole new model of philanthropy—a spare, lean, entrepreneurial model that employs leverage instead of largesse to make things happen," writes Geoffrey Cowley in a *Newsweek* cover story.[15]

AGENDA ITEM: BUSINESS LEADERS
SHOULD GIVE ADDED ATTENTION
TO ISLAMIC COUNTRIES

Since the September 11 attacks, Washington and its allies have increased their attention to the Muslim world. CEOs, too, need to think about the consequences to the global business environment if there is no alternative to Islamic fundamentalism. They can help create the economic conditions in which Islamic nations can plug into the global economy and take advantage of it to modernize their societies. There is no more complicated question or greater challenge facing world leaders, for real progress cannot proceed unless Islamic societies open their political systems, modernize their educational systems, and institute massive social reforms. And it's by no means clear that this will happen in the foreseeable future. Still, efforts to help Islamic countries become bigger and more prosperous participants in the world economy should proceed now, because economic liberalization can add to pressure for more political openness. A little is better than nothing. We have to hope that Islamic societies will eventually turn the corner. Anything else would be a cynical rationalization for not trying.

Numerous studies by The World Bank and Islamic organizations document the extent to which Islamic societies, particularly in the Middle East and North Africa, have failed to integrate themselves into the world economy. Plagued by lack of trade and investment, they have watched other nations grow while, with few exceptions, they have essentially stagnated. In the 1950s, per-capita income in Egypt was similar to that of South Korea; today it is just 20 percent of the South Korean figure. Saudi Arabia had a higher GDP in the 1950s than Taiwan; today, despite decades of substantial revenue from its oil sales, the Saudi GDP is half of Taiwan's. Morocco's per-capita income was close to that of Malaysia; now it is just a third. Islamic nations have about 20 percent of the world's population yet account for less than 6 percent of world trade and foreign direct investment. Given their exceptionally high birthrates, and that about half of their population is under twenty years old, without extraordinary measures to address their problems, the current prospect for Islamic countries is bleak indeed.[16]

How can CEOs help bring about change? Since a comprehensive attack on global poverty is in the interests of all Islamic countries, to the extent that business leaders assist on that account, they are already facilitating progress. Most of the poor Islamic nations are unable to take advantage of globalization, because they lack the tools. Multinational companies can make a contribution by promoting and supporting technical education in these countries— for example, by establishing computer centers inside their own facilities during downtimes, evenings, and weekends, and by providing incentives to qualified employees to act as mentors in local communities. We should not forget how much education goes on within MNCs. If a small amount of the effort to train employees is devoted to building up the communities in which these firms operate, it would become a powerful tool for progress. CEOs could establish special programs in their companies' home countries to train young local executives, paying their way. They could sponsor scholarships for advanced education at universities at home or abroad. They could work with Western universities to establish campuses in the Islamic world, where the faculty would come from local and foreign locations, and where the latest information technology could beam instruction from around the world throughout a particular country or region. Business leaders also can invite international lending institutions to join them in projects that improve local communities—particularly in areas in which multinational companies have exceptional competence, such as technological and managerial training.

Business executives could also press their home governments and those of Islamic nations in which they operate to get behind a policy agenda characterized by deregulation in Islamic countries and an expansion of foreign investment in them. Among the measures required are the reduction of state ownership of industry; the reduction of tariffs, quotas, and licensing arrangements that stifle industry and keep out foreign competition; and the dismantling of outside barriers to Islamic nations' exports. The Council on Foreign Relations has spelled out a thoughtful agenda for CEOs and heads of state alike. It pinpoints many obstacles to economic progress as seen by private businesses operating in the Middle East and North Africa. The key message is that neither domestic reforms nor more trade and foreign investment alone will be enough, but that they must proceed in tandem.[17]

A number of these activities are already in train. What is missing is a concerted effort by CEOs as a group acting in concert in the context of specific nations. The local U.S. Chamber of Commerce might guide such collective action in each Islamic nation. Alternatively, a number of countries have U.S.-government-supported Business Development Commissions that bring together the leaders of local and U.S. business communities in a partnership whose goals are to expand one another's business and improve the overall climate for investment. American ambassadors in countries ranging from the Sudan to Indonesia need to deepen their partnership with the heads of local U.S. companies. American business leaders, along with government officials and NGOs, could also take the lead in holding a series of conferences with their Islamic counterparts on a variety of issues critical to Islamic modernization—such as corporate governance, the creation of effective financial centers, and the building of productive workforces. The key concept is the kind of continuous engagement that leads to exchange of ideas, knowledge of constraints and opportunities, and trusted relationships.

In the end, development in the Muslim world will follow many paths. Islamic society stretches from Morocco to Indonesia and encompasses widely diverse states. Although no one would deny the political, social, and historical forces that make modernization so difficult for Islamic nations, a precondition is economic growth and development. And the investment, management, and technology that multinational companies can provide are essential.

Poverty provokes strong emotions on all sides of the political spectrum. The obligation of the rich to help the poor has been debated for generations and will not end in our lifetimes. The new urgency, however, is the growing integration of the world economy. The misery and despair in so large a swath of the globe's population now pose serious danger to everyone's welfare and security. Conversely, there are many positive opportunities if the lives of even some meaningful percentage of the billions living in poverty are substantially improved. No single policy will be decisive, but real progress cannot be made without large amounts of private investment. That, in turn, requires a level of participation by business leaders that has not yet been forthcoming, not only to drive that investment, but to help their foreign counterparts and their home and host governments establish the conditions in which investment will be effective. Now is the time.

CHAPTER 9

EXPANDING CORPORATE

CITIZENSHIP

F EW CEOS, IF ANY, would deny that corporations have obligations to be good citizens wherever they operate. At a minimum, that means a company should obey the laws of a country in which it does business. But since legal systems differ around the world, and since many developing countries have not established laws and enforcement mechanisms as elaborate as those in the United States or Europe, the definition of corporate citizenship on a global scale is anything but straightforward. The difficulty for many CEOs is encapsulated in this kind of thinking. "I operate in a hypercompetitive global marketplace. My primary responsibility is to be profitable in order to serve my shareholders. I have to obey the local laws, for sure. I must also follow the laws imposed by the country in which I am headquartered if they apply overseas. But if I go beyond that—if I pay wages or uphold environmental standards that are higher than legally required in a foreign country, and if that causes my company to be less competitive than my rivals and hence to be less profitable, am I doing the right thing?"

This kind of question reflects some intractable, real-world dilemmas. Suppose an American oil company is operating in Colombia, a country wracked by violence. The company hires security guards to protect its facilities. The service is effective in protecting the company, but it violates the norms of human rights in the United States—although not the de facto standards in the tough neighborhood in which it operates. What should an American CEO do? Consider another example: You are the CEO of a major American financial institution, and you are asked to bid on the financing of the Three Gorges Dam in China. The U.S. Export-Import Bank and the U.S. Overseas Private Insurance Corporation—arms of the U.S. government—have decided not to participate, having determined that the new dam will displace hundreds of thousands of people and damage the surrounding environment. But gaining closer relations with the government of China is a major strategic objective of your company, and participating in the underwriting of what may be the world's largest public financing project would be highly profitable and hence of benefit to your shareholders. You have also received reports prepared by consultants who say that building the dam would, over time, benefit millions of people in the region. How do you decide the right thing to do?

Differing perceptions of the power and obligations of multinational companies complicate the issues. From the standpoint of nearly all global CEOs, their companies have far less power than what governments and public pressure groups credit them with. These business leaders believe that only governments have the legitimate authority to make laws, enforce them, and cater to the social needs of their citizens—and the primary responsibility to do so. When host governments or pressure groups ask them to get involved in education, health, or the promotion of human rights—over and above the treatment of their own employees—the executives worry that they are undertaking something for which they have no mandate, no competence, and little time. They also fear being held responsible for results that are beyond their ability to deliver or control.

On the other hand, governments, international institutions, civic groups, and NGOs often see global companies as having more resources and influence—and a broader mandate—than corporate chief executives think they do. Governments and NGOs are frequently looking for these companies to be agents of social change and development in arenas in which the governments have failed.

Very few CEOs or members of their boards of directors have experience in managing, or the knowledge of how to manage, these contending viewpoints. But neither can they avoid dealing with them. They are under public pressure to get involved, and whatever they do or fail to do will be evaluated in a highly public way by a wide variety of groups. Equally important, as corporations struggle to recruit the most educated and talented men and women around the world, these companies' ability to be seen as being on the right side of progressive causes will become increasingly essential to their success. "If you want the best and the brightest," William Ford Jr., chairman and CEO of Ford Motor Company, told me, "then you have to build a company they can feel good about."[1]

There are no clear answers to the many dilemmas surrounding the question of what it means to be a good corporate citizen, and how this goal can be integrated with obligations to shareholders. But CEOs don't have the luxury of waiting while they and others figure out the answers. They operate in the here and now, and they must act today with the best knowledge and instincts they can muster. The imperative now is to give corporate citizenship more attention and higher priority, albeit in a careful way.

AGENDA ITEM: CEOS MUST BE PROACTIVE
AND TRANSPARENT WHEN IT COMES TO
ISSUES OF CORPORATE CITIZENSHIP
AND SOCIAL RESPONSIBILITY

The starting point for any business leader in navigating these swirling political and social currents is to have a clear idea of where the responsibilities of a company begin and end. Since there are few accepted international guidelines to rely on, CEOs and their boards need to make their own judgments. Although they will all begin with the idea that creating shareholder value is the sine qua non of the existence of a firm, they should define what else a company must do to create satisfied customers and productive employees who feel well treated. CEOs must also develop a philosophy that sets parameters on where corporate activity in a community begins and ends. This will never be a sharp line, but the best way to decide is to be in close consultation with host governments and community leaders, and to raise these questions to the level of boards of directors.

In other words, CEOs and their boards need a "true north"— a clear sense of who they are, what their company stands for, and what obligations it has, not only to shareholders but also to stakeholders around the world. These views should be clearly articulated to all constituencies—not as rhetorical mush, but as guidelines for operations. The purpose is to set realistic expectations for all concerned.

An excellent way to do this is to issue global corporate citizenship reports setting out a company's social philosophy, goals, efforts, and achievements. Among the companies that have pioneered these public statements are Ford, Royal Dutch/Shell Group, BP, and 3M Company. These documents compel a company to come to grips with difficult policies that they otherwise may put off or deal with haphazardly.[2]

Most multinational companies understand that once they are accused of being less than stellar citizens, they could be on the defensive for many years. The imperative therefore is to be ahead of the curve, to be positively engaged in key issues that arise for almost all companies—environmental protection, employee safety, and the like. A savvy company will appoint senior executives to monitor political and social pressures on the company, both on the local scene and internationally. These people will make it their job to learn about similar pressures on other global companies within and outside their own industries. They will be highly sensitive to political and social trends that could turn into anticorporate crusades. Had Monsanto Company been more alert, it might have avoided its serious setbacks in Europe over bioengineered foods. Had Coca-Cola been less insular, it might have avoided clashes with European governments over the safety of its products. Had Nike, Inc. recognized the significance of the antisweatshop movement, it might have avoided the huge shock to its brand that it experienced.

It's not enough to be actively engaged; companies need to be transparent about their goals, policies, and implementation strategies. In April 2001, for example, two American business associations, the Manufacturers Alliance and the National Association of Manufacturers, conducted a survey of forty-four companies to assess their policies on ethical, labor, and environmental standards in developing countries. It was filled with specific examples: All over the world, the Polaroid Corporation installs the same abatement equipment as on U.S. process lines; American Home Products requires its code of ethics to be signed by all its salaried employees, whatever the country they live and work in. The report concluded that "American manufacturers take their high standards with them, and are likely to raise, not lower standards in developing countries."[3] No doubt this is generally true, but companies will have to do much more than have the right policies in place. They will have to do more than just devise codes and write reports. The next stage in corporate citizenship—indeed, it has already arrived—is for companies to allow their community and social policies to be audited by represented third parties. This will require the development of a common framework for how to measure different kinds of progress, in place of the wide variety of measurement techniques that companies use now.

The importance of these social audits is rising quickly. They will insure that how a company defines its citizenship responsibilities is debated at its highest levels and is understood by all constituencies. Social audits will also demonstrate that CEOs are engaged in the communities in which their companies operate. And they will create widespread discussion about a company's social endeavors, giving that firm valuable feedback from a range of external constituencies. This in itself ought to help avert surprise political attacks on a company, because to the extent that explosive issues are looming, they will likely have been identified in advance.

Among the most important developments in the arena of social audits is the emergence of the Global Reporting Initiative (GRI), an international undertaking by a number of institutions and companies to develop voluntary guidelines for reporting on the economic, environmental, and social dimensions of their activities, products, and services. The effort began in 1997, and by April 2002 the GRI had established an independent international body to promote the guidelines and to continue to refine them. The GRI's reporting procedures are substantial. They relate to wages and benefits; labor productivity; job creation; environmental impacts of processes, products, and services; and social policies relating to workplace health and safety, labor rights, human rights, and working conditions at outsourced operations. The initiative "seeks to reduce confusion [and] harmonize rules of disclosure as much as possible."[4] The GRI sees itself as inaugurating a reporting system that parallels traditional financial accounting and eventually will achieve a similar level of comprehensiveness and precision. This serious effort will compel the attention of companies everywhere.

AGENDA ITEM: BUSINESS LEADERS SHOULD EXPAND THE WORK OF INDUSTRY ASSOCIATIONS

Consider the Fair Labor Association (FLA), a group formed by eleven leading apparel companies, including Nike, Patagonia, Inc., and Liz Claiborne Inc.; NGOs like the Lawyers Committee for Human Rights and the National Consumers League; and several universities. The purpose of the group is to eliminate sweatshops around the world. The members have developed a code that prohibits forced labor and child labor and supports freedom of association, minimum wages, limits on working hours, clean bathrooms, and similar rights and amenities. The group monitors one another's facilities abroad. It conducts surprise inspections. Companies in compliance with the group's code can put FLA labels on their products.

No one would say that the FLA is as thorough as it could be. But the template is a good one and ought to be extended to other industries. One sector ripe for this approach is mining, an industry in which many companies are realizing the advantages of improving their company image by setting minimal social and labor standards. Big mining companies are concerned that their access to financing could suffer because of banks' fears that their own reputations could be dragged down by association with companies that are the targets of social resentment. In early 2002, an industry working group known as Mining, Minerals and Sustainable Development met to consider industry guidelines on policies toward the environment, health and safety, ethical standards, and sharing information on best practices. The group is on the right course.[5]

Another industry that is thinking hard about its broader challenges is biotechnology. In the summer of 2002, Carl Feldbaum, president of the Biotechnology Industry Organization, told his 15,000-member audience that the industry needed to develop a "foreign policy" because it risked being dragged into a morass of social and ethical controversies in the developing world. The industry needed to learn from the mistakes of others and avoid them, he said. "Biotechnology will need much closer and more trusting relationships with foreign governments, the World Health Organization, and NGOs," he added.[6] Feldbaum, too, is on the right track.

Numerous other industry groups could work together, for by acting collectively, they would ensure that they would not reduce the competitiveness of any one company, while they would be working to enhance the overall welfare of society. As Roger L. Martin, dean of the Rotman School of Management at the University of Toronto, wrote in the *Harvard Business Review,* energy-producing companies could come together to create and implement a strategy to reduce greenhouse-gas emissions, and media companies could address the question of banning child pornography around the world.[7]

AGENDA ITEM: BUSINESS LEADERS SHOULD EXPAND ENGAGEMENT WITH PUBLIC AND NONPROFIT INSTITUTIONS

Business leaders need to step up their engagement with other organizations, public and private. A good case study is the Global Compact, initiated by U.N. Secretary-General Kofi Annan in July 2000 and signed by Nike, DaimlerChrysler, Royal Dutch/ Shell, and dozens of other companies, together with twelve labor associations and public-interest groups. The compact is a voluntary code aimed at improving human rights, eliminating child labor, and protecting the environment. Critics complain that because there are no sanctions for violations, the agreement is just rhetorical. However, the signatories have committed themselves to some important first steps, such as posting on their Web sites the progress made in implementing the principles and agreeing to a series of meetings to explore ways to promote the compact's goals.

Another example of an essential coalition is the code called Voluntary Principles on Security and Human Rights. In December 2000 U.S. Secretary of State Madeleine Albright and British foreign minister Robin Cook brought together Chevron, Texaco, Royal Dutch/Shell, and BP with various human rights organizations. The issue was how to balance the determination of companies to meet real security threats in dangerous places while still respecting human rights. The parties negotiated voluntary principles that companies would use to assess the impact of their activities on human rights; the relationship between companies and state security forces, both military and police; and the company relationships with private security forces. "The 'Voluntary Principles' address narrowly-defined issues, and the commitment of their participants remains untested," wrote Bennett Freeman, who helped negotiate the arrangement for the State Department. "But if this process continues and these principles stick . . . the negotiations may serve as a useful precedent as the old diplomacy of governments pushes into the still-virgin terrain of the diplomacy of globalization."[8]

Individual companies should partner with NGOs in many of their everyday activities that involve local communities. "It is a mistake sometimes reflected in media coverage to think that companies and NGOs are locked into an immutably hostile relationship," BP chief executive John Browne told an audience at

Chatham House in London in early 2002. "That isn't true. Companies benefit from scrutiny and challenge, and in some of the most complex areas in which we work the progress we can make is dependent on the cooperation and skills of NGOs." BP, for example, works closely with CARE and local NGOs in assisting communities in Colombia. It also works with the Red Cross to help displaced refugees in war-ravaged Angola and with the World Wildlife Federation to conserve the natural environment in Indonesia and Brazil. McDonald's works with Conservation International to prevent the loss of biodiversity—the loss arising from the practices of McDonald's agricultural suppliers around the world.[9] Nike, Gap, The World Bank, and the International Youth Foundation are working under the umbrella of the Global Alliance for Workers and Communities to improve the environment for workers on the entire supply chain that extends to countries such as Indonesia, Thailand, Vietnam, and China; included in their efforts is the provision of health care and education. American Express has been working with the Brazilian government and local professional institutes to help prepare young students for careers in travel and tourism.[10]

The idea of corporate partnership with NGOs and governments will become an ever bigger challenge for business leaders. When it comes to NGOs, for example, CEOs will need to develop a strategy every bit as sophisticated as those they apply to potential corporate partners. The number of NGOs is now vast—in the tens of thousands—and although some are only out to protest and disrupt corporate activities and globalization, most want to constructively solve problems. One task for business leaders is to identify with whom they can work, on both a global and a local level. In addition, they must realize that even the NGOs that are the most serious about working with multinational companies play a role much different from that of a company. NGOs are advocates for specific policies. They are not required to make the kind of trade-offs among a set of constituencies that CEOs must make. Under the best of circumstances, these partnerships will not be without serious disagreements, but they are crucial alliances, for each party brings essential skills and interests to a set of problems. Only through this kind of collaboration can the immensely complicated social issues be effectively addressed.

AGENDA ITEM: BUSINESS LEADERS SHOULD DEVELOP MORE RIGOROUS STRATEGIES TOWARD NGOS THAT ACT AS ANTIGLOBALIZATION PROTEST GROUPS

Ever since the 1999 demonstrations against globalization in Seattle, corporations and governments have been in disarray when it comes to responding to the overall protest movement itself. To be sure, developing a coherent strategy is difficult, given the wide range of NGOs that are involved and the disparate concerns they have raised. These concerns range from closing down The World Bank to promoting the human rights of women. The NGOs are well organized and well financed, and they have used the Internet to coordinate a much more effective public-relations campaign than have global companies, international institutions, or national governments.

The first part of a corporate strategy should entail the approaches already discussed: good corporate citizenship, partnering with constructive NGOs, and so forth. But this is not enough. NGOs have had too much of a free ride in identifying themselves with the public interest. They have acquired the high ground of public opinion without being subjected to the same public scrutiny given to corporations and governments. The danger is that they can too easily misrepresent facts and damage the reputations of other institutions without being held accountable.

It is time that companies and governments demanded more public examination of NGOs in order to hold them to the high public-interest standards the NGOs themselves espouse. Who makes the decisions in these organizations, how are these people selected, to whom are they responsible, and how are they held accountable? Who is providing the funding, and what are the interests of the financial supporters? Are the accounts audited and disclosed? In the United States, which NGOs are lobbying Congress, and if so, are they properly registered under the law? What is the track record of particular NGOs in terms of what they said they stood for, how they behaved, and what they achieved? Businesses and governments ought to press the media to ask these questions and relentlessly pursue the answers, just as the press does with regard to the private and public sectors. Since NGOs are pressing for transparency and accountability on behalf of multinationals and international institutions, it is only fair that they submit to the same standards. Were they to be forced to do so, the important debate about how globalization should proceed would become a lot more responsible and constructive. Some NGOs fully understand this. Irene Khan, who heads up Amnesty International, is one leader who does. "Accountability is important because of the power we have and the media exposure," she told the *Financial Times*. "We have to be as transparent as we expect governments and others to be."[11]

AGENDA ITEM: CEOS SHOULD PRESS GOVERNMENTS AND INTERNATIONAL ORGANIZATIONS TO DEVELOP GLOBAL RULES OF CONDUCT

Under any circumstance, the role of a multinational company in the society of any country will be both limited and ambiguous.

When the requisite laws and standards do not exist, business leaders are often being pressured to fill some of the void. But it would be far better for governments and international institutions to set and enforce the framework for global capitalism, because only governments have the authority and political legitimacy to do so. CEOs ought to be pressing public officials to move more urgently to establish stronger guidelines for wages, working conditions, environmental standards, anticorruption measures, and the protection of human rights and other such policies. The absence of good governance at the global and national level is an enormous liability for business leaders—among others.

I did not discuss some of the most critical issues related to corporate citizenship and social responsibility, especially environmental policy, only because I've tried to focus on more generic corporate policies. But this much should be said here: Every company needs an approach to environmental issues that is fully integrated with its business strategy. The challenge is big and the stakes are high. Moreover, for all the analysis, all the efforts of governments, public-interest groups, companies, and individuals, progress is slow at best. "It would be comforting to think that all the international negotiations, summit and conference agreements, conventions and protocols have at least got us to the point where we are prepared to act decisively—comforting but wrong," said James Gustave Speth, dean of the Yale School of Forestry & Environmental Studies at Oxford University. "Today the rates of environmental deterioration that stirred the international community twenty years ago continue essentially unabated. . . . The problems have gone from bad to worse."[12] Lest there be any doubt, this is the context in which the future challenges to business leaders and others must be understood.

In the future, the most effective global CEOs will give more attention to the relationships between their companies and the societies in which they operate. These executives will think about corporate citizenship and social responsibility, not just as philanthropy and good public relations, but as an integral part of their business strategy. They should be careful not to overpromise, but they should also not shy away from using their considerable energies and talents to invest in the full development of the society around them. Over the last few decades, a lot of progress has been made in the evolution of global corporate responsibility, but the thinking and the policies of corporate leaders and their government and NGO counterparts are still in the early stages. The importance of the challenge is matched only by its difficulty.

CHAPTER 10

INFLUENCING

FOREIGN POLICY

A MERICAN BUSINESS LEADERS need to take a greater interest in foreign policy. Business will be looking to Washington to keep the peace, for CEOs are anxious to avoid the
international conflicts that can severely disrupt a company's operations and undermine investor confidence. For American chief
executives in particular, global tensions bring another danger:
Given the rise of anti-American sentiment, the subsidiaries of U.S.
companies abroad are increasingly vulnerable to being singled
out and harmed. Chief executives also rely on Washington to
lead in the design of a global economy that is not only more open
but also governed by rules that are market-oriented and enforceable. And although business leaders may no longer expect the
United States to send in the marines to resolve a commercial dis-
pute, they do expect it to exert pressure behind the scenes, in
presidential communications and diplomatic exchanges.

Corporate America should also interest itself in foreign policy
because business will continue to be an instrument of it. The
most important and enduring relationships between the United
States and most other countries are often based on the trade
and investment of American businesses. Today, U.S. firms have

a significant presence in virtually every large country. They advise foreign governments on financial regulation, telecommunications policies, and the privatization of state-owned companies. These businesses are major employers, and they transfer critical capital, skills, and technology. They are transmission belts for American culture and values. Indeed, U.S. businesses often surpass the influence of American embassies on the societies in which they have become rooted. Not surprisingly, Washington needs business more than ever to reinforce foreign relationships.

Since the 1980s, CEOs have assumed that they could devote their efforts almost entirely to the internal operations of companies, leaving the pursuit of international relations to Washington. And why not? The United States emerged from the Cold War as the sole superpower; there were no big wars on the horizon; and trade barriers were dropping everywhere. There wasn't a lot to say to America's diplomats other than, "Keep up the good work." But American CEOs will now have to rethink much of what they took for granted about U.S. foreign policy. The global situation has changed radically.

President Bush came to Washington in January 2001 determined to follow a tougher, more unilateral foreign policy than President Clinton did. But by the afternoon of September 11, 2001, the administration had to rethink all its assumptions. Put simply, the war against terrorism became the new organizing principle for American foreign and national security policy. During the Cold War, the fault line for international relations was democracy versus communism. In the 1980s and 1990s, it was open versus closed economies. After the terrorist attacks, the United States established a new political divide: You were either part of the antiterrorist coalition, or you were a hostile regime. "What had been a drifting search for a foreign policy by a new Republican administration suddenly acquired a hard, overarching purpose, in which friends and foes were coldly redefined according to whether they were with the United States or against it," wrote Serge Schmemann in the *New York Times*. "Accusations of isolationism from frustrated allies have evaporated as the Bush administration probes every corner of the globe for allies."[1]

Overnight there were many big changes. Whereas the administration had been following a unilateral foreign policy— rejecting several foreign treaties relating to global cooperation on the environment and control of missiles, for example—it suddenly realized the need for a global coalition against terrorism. Although it had shown disdain for the U.N. as an organization, it now asked for and received the organization's support. By September 12, it was also clear that the United States would have to mount a major effort never before contemplated: intense engagement with the Islamic world. Inevitably, too, Washington had to think again about the kind of nation-building it had disparaged only weeks before, for weak states were breeding grounds for terrorists.

Washington also made an abrupt shift away from the primacy of economic relationships, back to the military links that characterized so much of the Cold War period. Through most of the 1990s, U.S. foreign policy had gravitated from the Departments of State and Defense and toward the Departments of Treasury and Commerce, as well as the Export-Import Bank and the overseas Private Investment Corporation. But with the declaration of the war on terrorism, the rules of the game changed. Months after the attacks on the World Trade Center and the Pentagon, the United States was playing some sort of military role in Afghanistan, Pakistan, the Philippines, Indonesia, and Yemen. It was developing military relationships with Uzbekistan, Kyrgyzstan, Georgia, and other states of the former Soviet Union. The Pentagon reclassified the war on drugs in Colombia as also a war on terrorism and was set to increase its military presence there. All this activity is being augmented by new cooperative arrangements between the Federal Bureau of Intelligence (FBI) and its counterparts in other countries, and between the Central Intelligence Agency (CIA) and other national intelligence organizations. The scope of American involvement seems almost limitless. "We will not send troops to every battle," said President Bush, "but America will actively prepare other nations for the battles ahead. If governments need training or resources to meet this commitment, America will help."[2]

It is hard to overstate the significance of a shift from economics and business to security and intelligence. During most of the Clinton administration, when business and economics were the leading edge of foreign policy, Washington gave priority to opening markets for trade and investment, to pressing other nations to establish transparent and fair regulatory processes, and to protecting intellectual property rights. The agenda was pushed by American ambassadors from Brazil to China and was further pursued by trade missions led by the secretaries of commerce and energy, and by visits from the secretary of the treasury and the chairmen of key regulatory agencies. America's goals were reinforced by its multilateral negotiations to conclude a series of major trade agreements, including the North American Free Trade Agreement, the Uruguay Round, and arrangements in particular sectors such as telecommunications and financial services. There was also a large-scale effort to establish bilateral business forums in countries like India and Turkey, in which American and foreign business leaders, working together, could pursue the promotion of trade and investment. When CEOs arrived in foreign countries, either alone or as part of high-profile trade missions, they were an important act in the ongoing play. A loose "America, Inc." was expanding its economic prospects.

A world in which the military, the CIA, and the FBI carry out the highest-priority relationships is considerably different. No one in the Bush administration would suggest that business and economics are less important than they were in the 1990s, but the new priority on security has, at best, diluted the high-level attention paid to them. In many societies, when key relationships are military-to-military (or between law enforcement and intelligence agencies), a renewed focus on security could easily resurrect the power of groups once known for their ultra-nationalist tendencies. The intensified cooperation between our intelligence agencies, though necessary, creates links that are nontransparent and ultimately nearly impossible to monitor and assess. In many countries, too, elites and ordinary citizens alike fear the CIA and its foreign equivalents. Perceiving that Washington is again in bed with these organizations, as it was during the Cold War, these foreign officials, businesspeople, and other citizens whom American companies would want to court abroad may become more suspicious of the overall intentions of any U.S. group, public or private. In this undercover world, agents can fight terrorism only by "terrorizing" the terrorists. It is a world in which the ends justify the means, in which human rights must often be suspended, in which those searching for terrorists are necessarily aligned with many unsavory people. These less-than-desirable elements represent the opposite kind of government official or business leader that American CEOs seek as partners. Although new U.S. allies can help the United States pursue an antiterrorist campaign, those relationships are unlikely to help in promoting open political and economic systems; in fact, just the opposite could happen.[3]

In this new world, the United States has to sort out how it will use its overwhelming power. U.S. military and economic strength far exceeds that of any other country. The nation spends more on defense annually than do the next nine countries combined. In 2002, President Bush proposed to increase Pentagon spending by an amount that exceeds the whole defense budget of any European nation. As Joseph Nye, the dean of Harvard's Kennedy School, points out, the United States is the only country possessing both nuclear weapons and conventional forces with global reach. According to Yale historian Paul Kennedy, in addition to its dominant role in global trade and investment, the United States accounts for a disproportionate amount of other assets. For example, 45 percent of all global Internet traffic takes place within its borders, and 75 percent of all Nobel laureates in the sciences and economics live in the United States.[4]

But how can the United States use this power so that it doesn't unleash resentment and backlash—as happened to other empires, from Rome to nineteenth-century Great Britain? Indeed, the biggest challenge Washington may face is to bring other countries along with it for the longer term. They include not only our traditional allies, Europe and Japan, but also influential regional powers, such as Russia, China, India, and Brazil. To build lasting coalitions, the United States will also have to decide on the proper balance between the use of brute military force on the one hand, and economic and social policies on the other. In the protracted battle against terrorism, the United States will be dealing with governments and people whose values conflict with its own. How can Americans accomplish this without undermining the rule of law that the nation has stood for since its inception?

In mid-2002, there were signs that the Bush administration was prepared not only to exercise its power but to embrace a new foreign-policy doctrine as dramatic in its implications as was the policy of containing communism after World War II. In addition their determination to fight terrorism, the president and members of the administration were also talking about punishing

countries that were building or hiding weapons of mass destruction. They said that America must do more than condemn and
contain these nations—that is, it must do more than prepare deterrence against their weapons. The nation, they contended, had
the right to go on the offensive and preempt the development
and deployment of those weapons. "I really think this period is
analogous to 1945 to 1947 when the containment doctrine took
shape," national security adviser Condoleezza Rice said in an interview with Nicholas Lemann of the New Yorker. In the same article, Richard Haas, a high-ranking State Department strategist,
mused on the administration's emerging ideas about the "limits
of sovereignty." When nations support terrorism "in any way," he
explained, they forfeited their sovereign independence. "This
can lead to a right of preventive, or preemptory, self-defense. You
essentially can act in anticipation if you have the grounds to
think it's a question of when, and not if, you're going to be attacked."[5] On June 1, 2002, at West Point, President Bush made
the point again. "If we wait for threats to fully materialize," he
said, "we will have waited too long. We must take the battle to
the enemy, disrupt his plans and confront the worst threats before they emerge."[6]

The new direction of American foreign policy goes to the heart
of the environment in which America's business leaders will be
operating for years to come. While the United States has no
choice but to fight terrorism with all the means at its disposal,
the danger of overstretching in the short term—of trying to be
everywhere, of using military means disproportionately, of intervening in foreign societies without understanding the consequences—could undermine rather than further American goals
in the long term. It certainly could play havoc with the global economy. During the Vietnam War, Senator William Fulbright talked
about the "arrogance of power." At the same time, Harvard political scientist Stanley Hoffman wrote about America's being tied

down by intractable foreign commitments, like Gulliver and the Lilliputians. Is the United States headed in this direction again?

Business leaders cannot make foreign policy or conduct it. Nor can they deal with all the issues I've mentioned. They have to pick areas in which they have competence and a central concern. But standing quietly on the sidelines and leaving all foreign policy to Washington is not in their interest or the public interest.

AGENDA ITEM: CEOS SHOULD PRESS FOR SUSTAINED MULTILATERALISM

Business leaders should be advocating that American foreign policy stay on the multilateral course that began on September 11. Given that the United States is a prime target for terrorists and is disproportionately powerful, no one ought to suggest that this country is merely one among equals: It has to protect its interests and it has to be prepared to do so alone if necessary. But it should also make maximum efforts to listen to other nations, consult with them, and cooperate where possible. This may sound too logical to belabor, but there are many reasons to feel that the administration will revert to the unilateral strategies with which it came into office. America's military success in Afghanistan could easily reinforce those tendencies, as could the sheer disparity of military power between the United States and everyone else.

The problem was on full display when, in his State of the Union speech on January 29, 2002, President Bush expanded the war on terrorism by designating Iraq, Iran, and North Korea as an "axis of evil" that threatened the peace of the world by developing weapons of mass destruction. Whether or not the policy was advisable in the first place, what was clear from the overseas reaction was that there had been no consultation or coordination on this critically important pronouncement with America's closest allies. Said Chris Patten, the European Union's commissioner for external affairs, "I hope those [unilateral] instincts will not prevail, because I believe them to be profoundly misguided. The lesson of September 11 is that we need both American leadership and international cooperation on an unprecedented scale."[7] Columnist Tom Friedman of the *New York Times* put it this way: "America will be the chef who decides the menu and cooks all the great meals and the NATO allies will be the busboys who stay around and clean up the mess."[8]

The new doctrine of preventive deterrence has further raised the concerns of American allies. Whatever its merits, it raises several profound questions of international law. If the United States determines that it is justified in preemptively attacking another country, does it alone decide that? Does it have some obligation to get the backing of the U.N. or NATO? These issues are not spelled out, but unless they are, the audacity of this variant of unilateralism could backfire politically abroad to the long-term detriment of the United States' broad interests.

Some defenders of the administration say that the charge of "unilateralism" is misleading because the United States creates different coalitions of nations for different problems. But shifting coalitions are not the same as stable alliances. They are opportunistic on all sides. They do not provide mutual support when important trade-offs are at stake. "Nations in a constant state of realignment make for a dangerous and unpredictable landscape," wrote *New York Times* reporter Christopher Marquis. "One trouble with such a world is that you can never be sure of [who your friends really are]."[9]

For CEOs, America's move toward unilateralism or to a strategy of constantly shifting coalitions could be a big problem. On many foreign policy issues they care about—those that underlie the foundation of the world economy—very little can be achieved without sustained multilateral cooperation. Business executives ought to be arguing that the United States can and should be the world's leader, proposing ideas, contributing human and financial resources, bringing together coalitions of countries—and that it cannot do everything on its own. America may be able to bomb a country into the Stone Age, but alone it cannot root out terrorists in the Islamic countries, or stop the production of weapons of mass destruction, or regulate global financial flows, or expand global trade, or protect the global environment, or eradicate the AIDS virus that is decimating so many developing countries. In all these cases, the United States needs extensive help from other governments and from private groups. If it makes policy without consulting its allies, then these countries will surely hedge their commitments of support for fear of being surprised again. If Washington does not address the concerns of others, how can it expect them to consider its needs? Senator Russell Feingold (D.–Wisc.) said it well in raising an objection to the abrupt way Washington pulled out of any commitment to an international criminal court. He wasn't supporting the court, just criticizing the American style of turning its back and walking away: "These steps actually call into question our country's credibility in all multilateral endeavors. As we continue to fight terrorism worldwide, we are asking countries around the globe to honor important commitments, to crack down on the financial and communications networks of terrorists and international criminals, and to share sensitive intelligence with the United States. This is not the right time to signal a lack of respect for multilateralism."[10]

CEOs ought to be making the case for maximum feasible multilateralism in a variety of ways. Many business leaders are associated with councils of world affairs, think tanks, and universities, and they ought to present their views in these forums and encourage public debate and more publications on the question of America's diplomatic style. Many have close contacts with top government officials; it would help if they took the time to explain their concerns in private conversations. And in their various business trade associations, they should precipitate conversations on the dangers of too much unilateralism as well.

There are some special opportunities now for business leaders to encourage a multilateral direction for American foreign policy. America's most important partners are the countries that constitute the European Union and NATO. America's economic interests with Europe—when you consider trade, investment, and other dimensions—dwarf any other region besides NAFTA; annual flows of two-way transatlantic trade and investment are approaching $1 trillion. Beyond that, the cultural and historical bonds are exceptionally deep. It is not possible to overstate the importance of U.S. links with Europe, nor the challenge of maintaining them in the face of differences that are emerging with regard to the war on terrorism, policies toward Iraq and the Middle East, and a wide range of major trade issues. The basic fact is that the United States is in a war—a global war. Europe is not. How much more fundamental can differences be? That said, business leaders should be pressing Washington to articulate a twenty-first-century vision of a transatlantic community, including deeper liberalization of trade, greater cooperation between regulatory agencies, and mechanisms to identify and resolve disputes at an early stage. At least these efforts could constitute a constructive and centrifugal force against growing political rifts.

America's incipient cooperation with Russia and China in the war against terrorism should also be expanded and intensified. Here is a singular opportunity to get the most influential nations in their respective regions under one tent. Business leaders ought to be contributing to a blueprint for integrating Moscow and Beijing into the international community via treaties and technical assistance to help those countries develop modern economies that are open, soundly regulated, and linked to the global economy. Beyond working with Moscow and Beijing, CEOs should spur a renewal of attempts to establish or to strengthen global frameworks for environmental protection, labor standards, the protection of intellectual property rights, the prevention of bioterrorism, the control of nuclear materials, the prevention of the spread of infectious diseases, and other global challenges.

AGENDA ITEM: CEOS SHOULD KEEP GLOBAL ECONOMIC PRIORITIES HIGH ON THE ADMINISTRATION'S RADAR SCREEN

Business leaders will have to lean against the prevailing political winds of the strong emphasis on national security. They could draw the attention of the administration, Congress, think tanks, and the public to problems that are festering in the world economy. The implosion of the Japanese economy, the likelihood of a rise in protectionism in much of Latin America, and the dangerous growth of the American trade deficit and its foreign debt are a few obvious examples.

Business leaders could also encourage congressional hearings on various global economic challenges. Their organizations could not only increase their lobbying for more open trade and investment policies but prepare and release reports on global economic issues that will grab the attention of Washington, the media, and the public. In the late 1960s, a bipartisan national commission was formed to look at the global economic challenges facing the United States. In the early 1970s, under the guidance of Secretary of Commerce Peter Peterson, the Nixon administration prepared a series of white papers on America's global economic agenda. As exceptionally clear explanations of why the United States needed to cooperate more closely with Europe, Japan, and Canada, the papers laid out a compelling rationale about the changing American interests in the world economy. CEOs could press for similar efforts that would center on the global financial and economic imperatives for the post–September 11 era.

Were similar studies to be conducted today, they would have to come to grips not just with countries or regions, or particular policies for finance and trade. The bigger question is the role of the only true superpower in the world economy. There are at least two critical issues deserving attention. The first is the relationship between military power on the one hand, and economic influence on the other. The administration seems to be operating on the premise that overwhelming superiority in the first category translates into the second. But that is by no means clear. Despite America's military prowess, there is no evidence that the nation has more influence over, say, European trade policy or economic reforms in Japan, than it has had for decades. In fact, one could make the opposite case: that resentment against U.S. power makes other countries even more reluctant to automatically follow American economic dictates. The implication is that the United States must pay far more attention to its economic and commercial policies.

The second problem is this: The Bush administration doesn't seem to acknowledge any special responsibilities accruing to the United States as a result of its overwhelming power. But if history shows us anything, it is that if a country is a hegemonic power, and if it wants to remain one, then it bears responsibility for maintaining the basic system of trade and finance. Not only must it take the lead in making the rules, but it must be their number one supporter, and it must get others to buy into them. It must strongly back international institutions, or they will not survive. It must use its strength to follow certain policies for the sake of the system as a whole—keeping its borders open to trade and immigration, and providing generous foreign aid. The United States does not act this way to the extent that it should. If it did, the administration would not have abandoned the Kyoto treaty, using the rationale that it was too costly for Americans. (The treaty may have been flawed, but at the least Washington could have proposed some constructive fixes or alternatives.) The administration would not have imposed high tariffs on imported steel, using the flimsiest of pretexts to cover up what was purely and simply a political sop to domestic interest groups. It would not have agreed to agricultural subsidies that made a mockery of its strident criticism of other countries' financial support for their farmers. It would not have played spoiler to virtually every international endeavor that wasn't invented in Washington. CEOs ought to be trying to change this situation, unless they want their companies to be on the receiving end of mounting resentment against an open world economy supported by the rule and law. "There is a race between the growing power of America and the growing complexity of the world," wrote columnist Dominique Moisi in the *Financial Times* in June, 2002. "But it is a race that America cannot win."[11]

AGENDA ITEM: CEOS SHOULD STEP UP SUPPORT FOR THE PROTECTION OF HUMAN RIGHTS AND DEMOCRACY

One of the great downsides of the war on terrorism is that the United States has had to accept help from nations that suppress human rights. In the interests of maintaining a coalition willing to supply air bases, share intelligence, and clamp down on the financial institutions that support terrorists, Washington has lowered the pressure it might otherwise have exerted on the human rights front. To make matters worse, several of America's new-found allies have used the war against terrorism to persecute domestic groups on the often dubious grounds that they are terrorists. American pressure on China to improve its human rights situation has subsided, even as Beijing escalates repression of dissident groups in its far-flung provinces like Xinjiang. The West has all but forgotten Russia's treatment of Chechnya. Tajikistan and Uzbekistan have traded bases for American silence about their denial of basic human rights to certain internal groups. Much the same can be said about Sudan, Egypt, Syria, and Saudi Arabia.

The human rights problem goes beyond America's looking the other way, to its active cultivation of relationships with repressive leaders. Take, for example, President Islam A. Karimov of Uzbekistan, who visited the White House in March 2002. Described by Todd Purdum of the *New York Times* as a "pariah-turned-ally," he was, only days before, publicly criticized by the State Department for his regime's pattern of torture, beatings, and arbitrary arrests, all under the pretense of fighting terrorism.[12] "The intellectual and political climate of a war on terror now resembles the atmosphere of the cold war," writes Michael Ignatieff of Harvard's Kennedy School. "Then the imperative of countering Soviet and Chinese imperial advances trumped concern for the abuses of authoritarianism in the western camp. The new element in determining American foreign policy is what assets—bases, intelligence, diplomatic leverage—it can bring to bear against Al Qaeda."[13] The problem may be even bigger than that, especially in Central Asia, where political stability is tenuous, economies are weak, and policies regarding health and education are primitive. As governments in the region appear increasingly repressive, the extremists among their populations could become energized, making the problems we saw in Afghanistan only the beginning of a massive political upheaval. "[These trends] are almost certain to destabilize these countries, sow strife in the region, and possibly target the U.S. just as the terrorist group Al Qaeda has," wrote Ahmed Rashid in the *Wall Street Journal*.[14]

CEOs should not welcome these trends, needless to say. Aside from the turmoil that could erupt in some countries, a government that exercises arbitrary power against people in one arena is likely to do the same in another. If a government suppresses human rights, then it will not allow for true economic freedom. It will be hostile to entrepreneurial activities; it will not allow people to invest where they choose; it will be lax in enforcing the intellectual property rights of individuals with original ideas; it will oppose freedom of expression and freedom of assembly—in short, it will put the state above the rule of law and above the freedom of its citizens. And, as the 1980s and 1990s have shown in Iran, Poland, Russia, the Philippines, and South Africa, repressive regimes are not stable ones; the chance of insurrection from within is increasingly likely as those who are repressed have access to news and resources from abroad. I'm not advocating that CEOs criticize other nations' human rights policies in a high-profile, public manner. But behind the scenes, they ought to be asking Washington the tough questions about its recent relationships with problematic regimes and the important values that risk being lost.

AGENDA ITEM: CEOS SHOULD HELP WASHINGTON WITH ITS PUBLIC DIPLOMACY

Business can encourage and assist Washington in getting America's message out accurately and quickly to millions of people abroad who are subject to local propaganda and other distortions of the truth. The countering of anti-American propaganda is an aspect of the war against terrorism, but it also is a much bigger issue.

Early on in the war against the Taliban, for example, it became clear that the United States had a big problem. "Incredible as it seems, according to Islamic experts, a mass murderer [Osama Bin Laden] seems to be winning the fight for the hearts and minds of the Muslim world," former U.N. ambassador Richard Holbrooke told the *Wall Street Journal* in October 2001.[15] His views were borne out in a Gallup Poll conducted four months later, which showed that in Islamic countries stretching from Morocco to Indonesia, respondents had overwhelmingly described the United States in terms such as "ruthless," "aggressive," "conceited," and "arrogant." They believed that the United States and the rest of the West had little respect for Islamic culture and religion, and they evinced a deep disrespect for Western nations, whose lifestyles they saw as undisciplined and immoral. Many in the Islamic world have concluded that the September 11 attacks were perpetrated by the United States or Israel, or at least that the attackers weren't Muslims. Naturally, these same respondents held a negative view of U.S. military action in Afghanistan.

A November 2001 study conducted by the Council on Foreign Relations identifies a number of steps that can be taken. These include more American broadcasting in Arabic of news and not propaganda; more "messengers" from outside the United States, especially credible Arab and Muslim interlocutors; the use of modern polling and opinion-gathering techniques applied to the Islamic world; and the creation of a Public Diplomacy Advisory Board that includes, among others, advertising and marketing executives with experience in the targeted countries. These are all important and necessary steps.[16]

But there is more. In the early 1960s, President Kennedy asked famed journalist Edward R. Murrow to head up the United States Information Agency (USIA), the information arm of the government abroad. Not only that, but Morrow was asked to sit in on the National Security Council Meetings, not just so he could understand the fundamentals of policies, but also so he could provide a viewpoint from the standpoint of how these policies would be received overseas. Business leaders should press for two things in this regard: First, the nomination and inclusion of a highly distinguished journalist to play this role, and second, the resurrection of a USIA for the twenty-first century, one that is a public-private venture with the private sector, that understands both the old and new medias, that relates not just to government leaders but to other constituencies such as foreign business leaders, young men and women, and schoolchildren. Another way that business leaders can help strengthen public diplomacy is to press the Bush administration and Congress for an expansion of foreign exchange programs at all levels—Americans going abroad and foreign nationals coming to the United States. Programs for high school students, college graduate students, teachers of all kinds, members of the media, midlevel government officials, doctors, lawyers, and so forth, would be the wisest long-term investment in the proper understanding of the complexity of the United States. By some measures, however, the funding for such programs has declined by one-third over the 1990s, so the trend has not only to be arrested, but redirected.[17]

To its credit, the Bush administration has showed its concern and started to work on America's image. By late February, it was discussing the establishment of a White House office to explain America's global policies. There was also talk of setting up a White House Coalition Information Center that would operate out of London and perhaps other cities, too.[18] One hopes that the effort will go well beyond the war against terrorism and include America's case for democracy and liberal capitalism—for America's vision of globalization itself.

But it is a monumental task to turn around the American image abroad. Even as the United States steps up its efforts, it will be difficult to keep up with the explosive growth of Arab media—TV, satellite, Web sites—that broadcast news from a highly prejudicial vantage point. It will be equally difficult to avoid the specter of Washington-sponsored propaganda, along the lines of its former cold war efforts. There is a risk, moreover, that the U.S. government will focus on input more than results, as governments often do. Charlotte Beers, undersecretary of state for public diplomacy, put it well to a gathering of CEOs at Yale in the spring of 2002. "It's not what you say, " she said, "it's what they hear."[19] No foreign policy challenge is more difficult now. "There is potentially decades of work to do," said Jim Wilkinson of the White House press operation.[20] He is dead right.

AGENDA ITEM: CEOS SHOULD PRESS FOR
A FOREIGN POLICY ADVISORY BOARD

American CEOs have a lot to contribute to the shaping of foreign policy. Many of them have been part of multinational management teams and have overseen a global work force. More than government officials, they have had to look at the world through the eyes of others. Whatever kind of international system emerges, American CEOs will be a central part of it, because most countries of the world still have as their highest objective economic growth and development, a central element of which is private foreign investment.

The Bush administration should establish a special business advisory board for international affairs that meets regularly with the cabinet and the president to review U.S. diplomatic strategy. It is important that this board not be attached just to the Department of State, for America's foreign relations go well beyond the areas of traditional diplomacy. The U.S. Treasury is a major actor in foreign policy, as are the Departments of Agriculture, Transportation, Justice, Commerce, Energy, and several regulatory agencies. (When it is established, the Department of Homeland Security will also be a player in foreign policy.) The board should therefore be advising the entire national security council. It would be especially useful in looking at the nation's international policies with a wide-angle lens and no bureaucratic stake in any one part of the government. It could be a force for thinking broadly and long-term, for integrating different strands of policy that often operate at cross purposes. Likewise, the board could supply the administration with something it doesn't often get— a collective view from the business world that supersedes the interest of any one firm or industry. The board would also serve an important purpose in the post–September 11 era: to help the administration think through the proper balance of regulation and openness in the world economy, including assessing the total impact of evolving security measures in finance, immigration, transportation, and cyberspace.

For most of the post–Cold War period, there has been a sense that American CEOs can get on with business free of the geopolitics of the past. Deregulation, privatization, and the lowering of trade and financial barriers were supposed to make governments less important and market forces more so. It was never that simple, however, and now, in what Secretary of State Colin Powell has called the post–*post*–Cold War period, it is clear that business needs to play an important role in formulating foreign policy. Greater involvement by CEOs would be a controversial move, but the terrorist attacks changed the scope and direction of U.S. foreign policy, and business leaders need to be part of the new world that is fast emerging.

CHAPTER 11

IMPROVING BUSINESS

EDUCATION

I N   T H E   W O R L D after September 11, 2001, and the world after the Enron scandals, the education of tomorrow's business leaders requires reexamination.[1] After all, future executives not only will need to be technically competent in the basics such as finance, marketing, and operations, but will require a knowledge of government—how it works, and how to work in partnership with it. They must also know more about the international organizations and NGOs. They should keenly appreciate and understand many aspects of global business: how to operate in a world of multiple jurisdictions with different political and legal systems and a multitude of cultures and customer preferences; the possibilities for, and the limitations of, the social responsibility of their companies at home and abroad; and how geopolitics affects their operations and their strategies. Future CEOs ought to possess a moral compass that allows them to reinject into the business culture much of the integrity that seeped away in recent years. For chief executives in the 1980s and 1990s, the premium was on an inward focus on the competitiveness and profitability of their companies. While these goals are still critical, they will no longer be enough. An understanding of the complex external environment will be just as important—and indeed a major element of achieving sustained financial success.

Today's system for educating business executives does not go far enough to train CEOs to be leaders in society. The educational process needs to be broader and to take place over a longer period. It needs to be aimed not only at a company's management but also at those who serve on the boards of directors. It needs to encompass not just M.B.A. curricula but executive education programs, too.

This is no small undertaking. In the United States, over 2,400 colleges and universities have business programs. Over 100,000 students are pursuing M.B.A. degrees, constituting 25 percent of all graduate students. Some of these business programs provide continuing education for employees. Companies themselves are also providing formal education for their own executives; General Electric's campus at Crotonville, New York, is perhaps the most famous and has become a model for many others, such as Motorola, PepsiCo, Goldman Sachs, Sun Microsystems, Inc., Johnson & Johnson, and Siemens.

It is not realistic to think that both the narrower technical requirements and the wider needs can be accommodated in the usual two-year M.B.A. program unless there is a total revamping of courses and teaching methods. In the ideal model, such issues as environmental sustainability, globalization, public policy, and business integrity would have to be fully integrated into each course. Professors' horizons and knowledge—generally highly specialized—would have to be greatly expanded, or else the faculty would have to combine their expertise and teach in teams. Even if business schools desired such innovations, the changes would take a decade or two to materialize. Short executive-education courses, as they are now constituted, do not cover the requisite ground either. A sampling of the course offerings at the nation's leading schools shows that they are too narrowly oriented; typical course titles include the following: Leading Fast Growth Companies, Consensus Building for Negotiation, Managing Your Global Supply Chain. Courses taught within companies also fall far short, dealing with challenges such as team building, the pooling of knowledge and experience, and the fostering of a culture of high performance with a company. In fact, because so much material in corporate universities is drawn from experience inside the company itself, these courses often reinforce the insularity of business leaders.

To be sure, the picture is not so black and white. At the M.B.A. level, a student can often expand his or her horizons with selected courses in other parts of a university. At Yale, M.B.A. students can do some of their work in law, international relations, and philosophy—all offered by other schools or departments. Similar op portunities exist at Harvard, Stanford, Duke, and many other top business programs. In a 2001 study, the Aspen Institute and the World Resources Institute pointed to a number of exceptional business school programs that give attention to environmental and social questions. The study identified Harvard, Yale, Michigan, and George Washington University, among others. But relative to the number of business schools, the field of excellence is small. "Companies face a multiplicity of challenges in evaluating the long-term impact of their business decisions," the report said. "They need managers with an ability to understand diverse cultural, social and political systems; to cope with vastly different infrastructure and resource issues; and to work with organizations such as the U.N., the World Bank, and NGOs. . . . Few MBAs are being trained to think about such things and few have the skills to successfully tackle these issues."[2]

Selective executive programs, such as those at The Wharton School at the University of Pennsylvania or the Kellogg School of Management at Northwestern University, also address a broader definition of business leadership. Some education conducted by companies is also noteworthy; in its leadership training courses, for example, BP deals with corporate responsibility and relationships with NGOs and governments. But the main point remains: When viewed as a national system, the American way of educating its business leaders falls short of what CEOs and their boards of directors will need.

The last thorough examination of American business education was conducted by the Ford Foundation and the Carnegie Corporation of New York in the late 1950s and early 1960s. Both institutions issued sharp indictments, pointing to a lack of both academic legitimacy and professional relevance. Entrance requirements were too low, they said; faculty research was of poor quality; and the courses were too specialized and prepared students for entry-level positions rather than the challenges of a long career.

Many of the Ford and Carnegie recommendations were implemented by schools around the United States. In the intervening years, there have been a number of further innovations. In my seven years at the Yale School of Management, for example, we and our peer schools have wrestled with how to equip students with a true global perspective on business; how to integrate new information technology into business strategy and operations; how to link sound business management principles not only to profit-making enterprises but also to nonprofit institutions and government agencies—to cite just a few examples.

Now there is a need to make business education more relevant to the post–September 11, post-Enron world. The issue is what kind of education ought to be made available over someone's entire career. Most business education is centered on what an individual must do to succeed, whether in climbing the corporate ladder or in starting a new enterprise. Rarely does it ask the question, What does society require from its business leaders? This is a dangerous omission. After all, if the issues I have discussed in this book have any significance, it should be clear what kind of broad contribution business leaders will need to make to the future of our society. In a world of increasing violence, we ought to look to them to keep up the drumbeat for economic progress and development. In a world in which government power is expanding, we should look to top corporate executives to push for promarket regulation. In a world where hundreds of millions of people are investing in markets for their future security, we have a right to expect that business leaders see themselves as stewards for the future. Business education ought to be dealing with *both* the development of the individual and the needs of the nation and the global economy

AGENDA ITEM: BUSINESS LEADERS SHOULD PUSH FOR THE ESTABLISHMENT OF A NATIONAL COMMISSION TO TAKE A FRESH LOOK AT BUSINESS EDUCATION AT ALL LEVELS

As part of evaluating business education, the business world would benefit from a national commission that could approach the issue from all angles and at all levels. This effort could be modeled on the work of Ford and Carnegie in the 1950s. The terms of reference should go beyond M.B.A. programs to the multiple educational levels that exist, what they should accomplish, and who should attend. We also need an examination of the training that business faculty receive and the research they do, to assess both coverage and relevance. While the members of the commission ought to include business leaders, it must also have representation of other parts of society—legislators, labor leaders, scholars from outside the business-school community. The question before the group can be simply stated: If the goal is to prepare CEOs for responsible leadership in this new century, what can we do to improve the system we now have? A few areas that ought to be part of the investigation follow.

How should schools be evaluated?

M.B.A. programs are heavily driven by the ratings awarded by *Business Week, U.S. News & World Report,* the *Wall Street Journal,* and the *Financial Times.* These publications use different criteria—the test scores of incoming students, starting salaries for graduates, attitudes of corporate recruiters about the school, views of recent alumni about how well the school has prepared them, teaching quality as rated by students. There are few, if any, metrics that would measure how schools are preparing society's future leaders—men and women who understand the role of corporations in the world at large, who will be far less likely to make the mistakes that executives of Enron and Arthur Andersen made, and who would grasp the private-public challenge inherent in an age of terrorism. Many deans and professors (myself included) would agree with Jerold L. Zimmerman of the Simon School of Business at the University of Rochester:

> U.S. business schools are locked in a dysfunctional competition for media ratings. This ratings race has caused schools to divert resources from investment in knowledge creation . . . to short-term strategies aimed at improving rankings such as [focusing on] placement offices and public relations campaigns. Curriculums are narrowing and [they are] training students for their first jobs, not their entire careers.[3]

The commission ought to examine not only the optimal rating system for M.B.A. programs but also all kinds of executive education. In the latter case, media evaluations have been highly subjective and based almost entirely on customer satisfaction surveys—hardly a rigorous analysis of what business and society at large needs.

What do top executives and board members need to know about accounting, law, and business integrity?

There is a strong case for specialized ongoing programs for business leaders while they are in their jobs. As the Enron case shows, it is not enough to say, "The accountants and lawyers said it was OK." The extraordinary complexity of financial reporting and business law compels a clearer definition of the precise responsibilities of CEOs and their boards (see detailed discussion in relation to Enron, Arthur Andersen, and Merrill Lynch in chapter 5). The current system of business education, in all its dimensions, does not give enough attention to these challenges.

How should business education deal with the growing number of businesses in which the CEOs face conflicts between profitability and social goals?

These instances will increase as a result of hypercompetition and globalization. In finance, we have seen the conflicts that can arise when Wall Street firms try to serve both the companies whose securities they underwrite and the investors to whom they sell these same securities. In the media industries, there is an inherent conflict between maintaining standards of objective journalism and enriching the shareholders, who might well do better when the news comprises salacious entertainment. In the pharmaceutical industry, some of the many conflicts come with the tension between high prices and affordability, but the ethical dilemmas surrounding businesses in the biosciences are only now coming into focus. Nowhere in America are future executives being well prepared to deal with these sorts of issues.

How should business education encompass global corporate citizenship?

Students and professors ought to be familiar with good practices and bad, as should CEOs and their boards. We need more case studies and more research, but the book is being written in the field today, so schools must also find a way to tap into real-time experience. Moreover, employers should give more emphasis to recruiting M.B.A. graduates who evidence understanding of the imperative to integrate financial performance with a socially responsible, long-term strategy. This rarely happens now. As the authors of "Beyond Grey Pinstripes 2001" say: "Clearly, a double disconnect is at play, a disconnect between the skills businesses say they need, the skills MBAs are being taught, and the skills businesses look for in campus recruiting efforts."[4]

How can business leaders gain a better appreciation for the interaction of business, government, and nonprofit organizations?

CEOs need to know how these other institutions are structured and what drives their strategies and policies. They should also understand how to better communicate with them and how to structure creative partnerships. All this is plowing relatively new ground, to be sure. Yet effective approaches can open new opportunities for companies to prosper amid rapidly changing economic and political conditions, and, alternatively, strategic mistakes could severely damage a company's reputation.

These questions are just a starting point for a vigorous debate over how business leaders should be prepared for the external challenges they will encounter, challenges that go to the heart of the business agenda for the years ahead.

In the post–September 11, post-Enron world, business leaders will be facing an unusually complex environment. For decades, market forces and entrepreneurial energies have been unleashed and have created a vast global economy closer to free-market ideals than anything today's CEOs have known. Now more than ever, business should find itself able to get on with its job, free from the regulatory encumbrances that characterized previous eras. But that is not the complete picture. September 11 and Enron ushered in new and urgent considerations of national security and market integrity. And they came along at the same time that economic globalization was outstripping the ability of governments to create the necessary foundations of laws and institutions. All these developments have combined to radically expand the agenda for business leaders. The territory is uncharted, and the challenge—because it is on so many fronts—is unprecedented. Business education needs to rise to the occasion.

CHAPTER 12

THE CHALLENGE AHEAD

B Y JULY 2002, just several months after the September 11 terrorist attacks and the Enron debacle, the broad context for American policies was in significant flux. There were questions about the adequacy of U.S. preparations for homeland security. There were signals that the next stage in the war against terrorism would be an American invasion of Iraq, with highly uncertain long-term consequences. Corporate malfeasance was being blamed for a lack of investor confidence and thus for contributing to a stock market that had lost several trillion dollars in value since its high point in March 2000. The rapidly declining market threatened to set back prospects for growth in the United States, and concerns were mounting that the very foundations of our shareholder culture abroad rested on increasingly weak foundations. Serious budget deficits loomed for years to come and foreshadowed a potential return of the financial and policy tensions of a decade ago. Momentum for global trade negotiations had slowed to a crawl, the value of the dollar was dropping in world markets, and at least two continents—Africa and Latin America—were experiencing deep economic reversals. For all the talk about the need to mount a full-fledged attack on global poverty, real evidence of policy movement was hard to find. And when it came to U.S. foreign policy, Washington's relations with its allies were increasingly strained by charges from other governments that the United States was acting without reference to their concerns.

Nevertheless, there was much constructive ferment. The blueprint for a new Department of Homeland Security was proceeding rapidly through Congress, and President Bush set forth his first comprehensive plan for combating terrorism at home. Legislation to deal with several aspects of corporate transgressions—including the most sweeping overhaul of accounting laws since the 1930s—passed with overwhelming support. The SEC was pledging much tougher surveillance over companies and CEOs. The stock exchanges were moving to elevate the standards for corporate governance. Despite all the political and economic turmoil, economic growth in the United States was holding up, productivity remained high, and inflation was almost nonexistent.

Indeed, the fundamental challenges of the post–September 11, post-Enron age were just coming into focus. Our society had entered a new era in which business and government would be forced to find a new balance vis-à-vis one another—not the unrestrained exuberance for free markets of the last two decades, and not heavy-handed government regulation, either, but hopefully something in-between.

While it will take years for new, sustainable arrangements to evolve, it is my hope that top business executives will be able to refurbish their severely tarnished reputations and help lead the way toward sounder public policies for their companies, their nation, and the global economy. I'd like to believe that they will understand that their responsibilities begin with building great institutions that serve shareholders for the long term, for that is the sine qua non for everything else they might do that has lasting value. But I hope they also construe their jobs to include more attention to employees, customers, suppliers, and communities. I hope that they realize that society at large is also a stakeholder, and that it is desperate for enlightened business leadership in shaping vital policies.

I've tried to make the case that the new era ahead demands a level of public engagement from our business leaders that we have not seen in half a century. It is not at all clear that there is a collective will among top executives to make the necessary changes, not clear that they will see this as their mission, not clear that they will feel they have the time, not clear that they will have the right skills and experience. But the United States and the world would be much worse off—and so would the global companies that are so important to our lives—if our leading businessmen and women didn't at least try.

For many of the facts and events in this book, I have relied heavily on the *New York Times*, the *Wall Street Journal*, the *Financial Times*, *Business Week*, *Fortune*, and *The Economist*. I have cited these sources whenever I felt it was important to do so, but I could not do complete justice to all the ideas that I developed from the excellent and thoughtful analysis contained in these publications.

CHAPTER 1: A NEW WORLD

1. "The Future of the State," *The Economist*, 18 September 1997, on-line edition, <www.economist.com>.

2. Andrew S. Grove, *Only the Paranoid Survive: How to Exploit the Crisis Points That Challenge Every Company and Career* (New York: Currency/Doubleday, 1996).

3. "Fallen Idols," *The Economist*, 2 May 2002, online edition, <www.economist.com>.

4. David Leonhardt, "The Imperial Chief Executive Is Suddenly in the Cross Hairs," *New York Times*, 24 June 2002, p. 1.

5. Anna Bernasek, "The Friction Economy," *Fortune*, 18 February 2002, p. 104.

6. Lee Walezak, "America's Biggest Job," *Business Week*, 10 June 2002, p. 34.

CHAPTER 2: PRECEDENTS FOR LEADERSHIP

1. Robert Nathan, quoted in Karl Schriftgiesser, *Business and Public Policy* (New York: Prentice Hall, 1967), p. 3.

2. For information about the CED, I have drawn heavily on two books by business historian Karl Schriftgiesser: *Business Comes of Age: The Story of the Committee for Economic Development and Its Impact upon Policies of the United States, 1942–1960* (New York: Harper & Brothers, 1960); and *Business and Public Policy*. I also drew on John B. Judis, *The Paradox*

of American Democracy: Elites, Special Interests, and the Betrayal of Public Trust (New York: Routledge Press, 2001), pp. 59–79.

3. Schriftgiesser, *Business Comes of Age*, p. 3.

4. Ibid., 21.

5. Judis, *The Paradox of American Democracy*, p. 67.

6. Diane B. Kunz, *Butter and Guns: America's Cold War Economic Diplomacy* (New York: Free Press,1997), p.32.

7. For background on the Marshall Plan, I used Kunz, *Butter and Guns,* and Michael J. Hogan, *The Marshall Plan: America, Britain, and the Reconstruction of Western Europe, 1947–1952* (Cambridge: Cambridge University Press, 1987).

8. Albert O. Hirschman, *Shifting Involvements: Private Interest and Public Action* (Princeton, NJ: Princeton University Press, 1982).

9. Arthur M. Schlesinger Jr., *The Cycles of American History* (Boston: Houghton Mifflin, 1986), p. 255.

10. Richard Tompkins, "Back to the Future," *Financial Times*, 3 November 2001, Weekend Section, p. I; and Roger Rosenblatt, "Back into the Fray of History," *Time*, 12 November 2001, p. 106.

11. Jack Welch, interview with author, 10 July 1999.

12. George W. Bush, State of the Union address, 29 January 2002; George W. Bush, remarks given at the Malcolm Baldrige National Quality Award ceremony, 7 March 2002. Speeches available at <www.whitehouse.gov>.

CHAPTER 3: REBUILDING THE REPUTATION OF CEOS

1. "Fallen Idols: The Overthrow of Celebrity CEOs," *The Economist*, 2 May 2002, online edition, <www.economist.com>; and "Plenty," *Business Week*, 13 May 2002, online edition, <www.businessweek.com>.

2. Alex Berenson, "The Biggest Casualty of Enron's Collapse: Confidence," *New York Times*, 10 February 2002, online edition, <www.nytimes.com>.

3. The *CFO* survey is described in Daniel Altman, "The Taming of the Finance Officers," *New York Times*, 14 April 2002, online edition, <www.nytimes.com>.

4. Ibid.

5. Marcia Vickers et al., "The Betrayed Investor," *Business Week*, 25 February 2002, p. 105; and Aaron Bernstein et al., "Bracing for a Backlash," *Business Week*, 4 February 2002, p. 33.

6. John Harwood, "Public's Esteem for Business Falls in Wake of

Enron," *Wall Street Journal,* 11 April 2001, online edition, <www.wsj.com>.

7. Stephen Labaton, "Downturn and Shift in Population Feed Book in White Collar Crime," *New York Times,* 2 June 2002, p. 1.

8. Charles Niemeir, quoted in Susan Pulliam, "SEC Broadens Accounting-Practices Inquiry," *Wall Street Journal,* 3 April 2002, online edition, <www.wsj.com>.

9. Michael Sesit et al., "Stock Bubble Magnifies Changes in Business Mores," *Wall Street Journal Europe,* 20 June 2002, p. 1.

10. David Woodruff, "Chief Executives Suffer Diminished Reputations," *Wall Street Journal Europe,* 17 June 2002, p. 1.

11. For background on Enron's political influence, there is extensive press reporting, including Deborah McGregor, "Enron Boost for Party Funds Reform," *Financial Times,* 16 January 2002, p. 6. In March 2002, the extent of Enron's political contributions were being "restated" upward, and the true total may not emerge for some time.

12. Arthur Levitt, quoted in Jane Mayer, "The Accountants' War," *New Yorker,* 22 April 2002, p. 64.

13. John A. Byrne, "Restoring Trust in Corporate America," *Business Week* (European edition), 24 June 2002, p. 37.

14. For background on Microsoft's government affairs operation, I drew on Jeffrey H. Birnbaum, "How Microsoft Conquered Washington," *Fortune,* 29 April 2002, online edition, <www.fortune.com>.

15. For background on the energy industry's political influence, see Dan Van Natta Jr., "Bush Policies Have Been Good to Energy Industry," *New York Times,* 21 April 2002, p. 22; and Laura Cohn, "The Energy Lobby Hits Pay Dirt," *Business Week,* 29 April 2002, online edition, <www.businessweek.com>.

16. From a speech by Henry Paulson, Jr., "Restoring Investor Confidence: An Agenda for Change," 5 June 2002, <www.gs.com>.

17. Emily Thornton and David Henry, "Big Guns Aim for Change," *Business Week* (European edition), 24 June 2002, p. 43.

18. David Leonhardt, "The Imperial Chief Executive Is Suddenly in the Cross Hairs," *New York Times,* 24 June 2002, p. 17.

19. Edward J. Markey, quoted in David E. Rosenbaum, "Since September 11, Lobbyists Use New Pitches for Old Please," *New York Times,* 3 December 2001, p. B3.

20. Bruce Nussbaum, "Can You Trust Anybody Anymore?" *Business Week,* 28 January 2002, online edition, <www.businessweek.com>.

21. John Harwood and David Rogers, "How New Legislation to Curb 'Soft Money' Might Redirect Power," *Wall Street Journal*, 15 February 2002, p. 1.

22. Bloomberg News, "O'Neill Condemns Corporate Scandals," *New York Times*, 24 June 2002, p. C2.

23. Joseph Nocera, "System Failure," *Fortune*, 24 June 2002, p. 64.

CHAPTER 4: PROTECTING THE HOMELAND

For much of the factual information on what is happening in the homeland security arena, I am greatly indebted to Intellibridge, a consulting firm in Washington, DC, that produces a daily report on homeland security developments, which I have received by e-mail. I have also drawn information from the Web sites of the Office of Homeland Security in the White House, the Council on Foreign Relations, and the Brookings Institution.

1. Hendrick Hertzberg, "Tuesday, and After," *New Yorker*, 24 September 2002, p. 27.

2. Tom Ridge, remarks to the Electronic Industries Alliance, Washington, DC, 23 April 2002, <www.whitehouse.gov>.

3. Dick Cheney, remarks at the New York Council on Foreign Relations, 15 February 2002, <www.cfr.org>.

4. For background on insurance costs, see David Hale, "Insuring a Nightmare," *World Link Magazine*, March/April 2002, p. 21.

5. Stephen E. Flynn, "The Unguarded Homeland," in *How Did This Happen? Terrorism and the New War*, ed. James F. Hoge and Gideon Rose (New York: Public Affairs, 2001), p. 183.

6. Ralph W. Shrader and Mike McConnell, "Security and Strategy in the Age of Discontinuity: A Management Framework for the Post–9/11 World," *Strategy + Business* 26 (January–February 2002): p. 32.

7. Tom Ridge, remarks to the Electronic Industries Alliance (see footnote #2 above).

8. For background on the Booz • Allen & Hamilton war game, see Gary Ahlquist and Heather Burns, "Bioterrorism: Improving Preparedness and Response," summary report (New York: Booz • Allen & Hamilton, undated).

9. C. Michael Armstrong, address to the McGraw-Hill Homeland Security Summit, Washington, D.C., 6 June 2002, <www.att.com>.

10. For background on the Disaster Response Network, see World Economic Forum, "World Economic Forum Announces Disaster Response Network," statement released by World Economic Forum in New

York, 2 February 2002; also supporting documents furnished by Parsons Brinckeroff, 506 Carnegie Center Boulevard, Princeton, NJ, 08450.

11. See "President Bush to Appoint Following Individuals to Serve as Members of the President's Homeland Security Advisory Council," 11 June 2002, <www.whitehouse.gov>.

12. Brookings Institution, "Homeland Security: New Brookings Study Analyzes Bush Administration's Proposals, Recommends Additional Steps," 30 April 2002, Brookings Institution Web site, <www.brook.edu>.

13. Jane Harman, quoted in Brookings Institution, "Homeland Security."

14. Jeffrey Rosen, "Spy Game," *New York Times Magazine,* 14 April 2002, pp. 46, 48.

15. David J. Rothkopf, "Business vs. Terror," *Foreign Policy,* May/June 2002, p. 56.

16. Phil Anderson, quoted in Yochi J. Dreazen, "Spreading the Wealth," *Wall Street Journal,* 28 March 2002, p. R7.

17. For information on U.S. vulnerability to the concentration of manufacturing in China, see the U.S. General Accounting Office, "Export Controls: Rapid Advances in China's Semiconductor Industry Underscore Need for Fundamental U.S. Policy Review," April 2002; Barry Lynn, "Unmade in America," *Harper's,* June 2002, p. 33; Jeffrey E. Garten, "China in the WTO: Let's Cut It Some Slack," *Business Week,* 8 October 2001, online edition, <www.businessweek.com>.

CHAPTER 5: RESTORING INTEGRITY TO MARKETS

1. For background on scandals, see Clifton Leaf, "Enough Is Enough," *Fortune,* 18 March 2002, pp. 62–64.

2. Harvey Pitt, SEC chairman, quoted in Andrew Hill and John Labate, "A Reluctant Street Fighter," *Financial Times,* 12 May 2002, p. 7.

3. John A. Byrne, "How to Fix Corporate Governance," *Business Week,* 6 May 2002, p. 69.

4. On changing the way CEOs deal with Wall Street, see Joseph Fuller and Michael Jensen, "How to Keep Your Stock Price Low," *Wall Street Journal,* 31 December 2001, p. A8.

5. Stephen Butler, speech to Cambridge Energy Research Associates Conference, Boston, MA, 13 February 2002.

6. Roy Smith and Ingo Walter, "Capitalism Will Clean Itself Up," *Financial Times,* 12 April 2002, p. 13.

7. In the section on stock options, statistics and quotes are from

Gregg Hitt and Jacob M. Schlesinger, "Stock Options Come under Fire in Wake of Enron's Collapse," *Wall Street Journal,* 26 March 2002, p. 1.

8. Statistics on the ratio of CEOs' to average workers' pay comes from "CEOs: Why They Are So Unloved," editorial, *Business Week,* 22 April 2002, online edition, <www.businessweek.com>.

9. John C. Whitehead and Ira M. Millstein, "Proposal for Legislation," letter to Steven B. Harris, Senate Committee on Banking, Housing and Urban Affairs, 2 April 2002, <www.senate.gov/~banking>.

10. John C. Bogle, "Has Corporate Governance Let Us Down?" *The Corporate Board* XXXIII, no. 134 (May/June 2002): pp. 8-10.

11. Ibid.

12. Simon Targett and Tony Tassell, "Institutions Draw Up Plans to Tackle Corporate Greed," *Financial Times,* 24 June 2002, p. 17.

13. David Komansky, quoted in Patrick McGeehan, "Merrill Chief Is Apologetic over Analysts: One Dismissed," *New York Times,* 27 April 2002, p. C1.

14. David Komansky, interview by Maria Bartiromo, *Market Week with Maria Bartiromo,* CNBC, 29 April 2002 (transcript).

15. James O'Toole, "Spreading the Blame at Andersen," *New York Times,* 26 March 2002, p. A25.

16. Alan Greenspan, remarks at the Stern School of Business, New York University, 26 March 2002.

CHAPTER 6: PRESERVING ECONOMIC SECURITY

1. For 2001 and 2002 budget statistics, see U.S. Congressional Budget Office, "The Budget and Economic Outlook," 23 January 2002.

2. George W. Bush, State of the Union address, 29 January 2002, available at <www.whitehouse.gov>.

3. "The Washington Budget Box," editorial, *New York Times,* 22 April 2002, p. A28.

4. The Concord Coalition, "Report on Fiscal Responsibility," June 2002, <www.concordcoalition.org>.

5. For health-care statistics, see Robert Pear, "Propelled by Drug and Hospital Costs, Health Spending Surged in 2000," *New York Times,* 8 January 2002, p. A14; Robert Pear and Robin Toner, "Amid Fiscal Crisis, Medicaid Is Facing Cuts from States," *New York Times,* 14 January 2002, p. 1; Ron Winslow, "Health Debate Emerges as Costs Rise Again," *Wall Street Journal,* 17 December 2001, p. 1; Reed Abelson, "Hard Decisions

for Employees as Costs Soar in Health Care," *New York Times,* 16 April 2002, p. C1.

6. David Broder, "Fix Health Care Now," *Washington Post,* 6 January 2002, p. B7.

7. Peter Landers, "Industry Urges Action on Health Costs," *Wall Street Journal,* 11 June 2002, p. A3.

8. George W. Bush, quoted in Alison Mitchell, "Social Security Pledges May Haunt Both Parties," *New York Times,* 6 February 2002, p. A18.

9. Paul Krugman, "Could've Been Worse," *New York Times,* 28 December 2001, p. 19.

10. For background on private pensions, see Edward Wyatt, "Pension Change Puts the Burden on the Worker," *New York Times,* 5 April 2002, p. 1.

CHAPTER 7: SUSTAINING FREE TRADE

1. Paul Volcker, statement before the U.S. Senate Committee on Banking, Housing, and Urban Affairs, 14 February 2002, <www.senate .gov/~banking>.

2. Daniel Yergin, interview with author, 15 March 2002.

3. Somini Sengupta, "U.N. Report Says Al Qaeda May Be Finding New Ways to Finance Terror," *New York Times,* 23 May 2002, p. A14; also Karen DeYoung and Douglas Farah, "Qaeda Assets Now in Commodities, Not Banks, Officials Say," *International Herald Tribune,* 19 June 2002, p. 4.

4. For background on efforts to clamp down on terrorists' finances, selected sources include the following: Kenneth W. Dam, Deputy Secretary of the Treasury, Testimony before the Senate Banking Committee, 29 January 2002; Edward Alden, "Complex Finances Defy Global Policing," *Financial Times,* 21 February 2002, p. 5; Charles M. Sennott, "Financial Regulators Seize Momentum of War on Terrorism," *International Herald Tribune,* 2–3 February 2002, p. 11; Michael M. Phillips, "G-7 to Call for a Police Network to Track, Cut Off Terror Funding," *Wall Street Journal,* 15 April 2002, p. A4; Glen R. Simpson and Jathon Sapsford, "New Money Laundering Rules to Cut Broad Swath in Finance," *Wall Street Journal,* 23 April 2002, p. 1.

5. Tony Judt, "America's Restive Partners," *New York Times,* 28 April 2002, section 4, p. 15.

6. "Tougher Policies on Refugees," editorial, *New York Times,* 18 February 2002, p. A18.

7. For background on airlines' coordinating databases, see Robert

O'Harrow Jr., "Fliers' Private Lives Face New Screening," *International Herald Tribune,* 2–3 February 2002, p. 1.

8. Moises Naim, "The Diaspora That Fuels Development," *Financial Times,* 10 June 2002, online edition, <www.ft.com>.

9. "Dangerous Activities," *The Economist,* 9 May 2002, online edition, <www.economist.com>.

10. For information on food inspections, see Robert Pear, "Food Industry's Resistance Stalls Bill to Protect Food," *New York Times,* 16 April 2002, p. A22.

11. "Dangerous Activities."

CHAPTER 8: REDUCING GLOBAL POVERTY

1. Poverty statistics come from the United Nations, "Report of the High-Level Panel on Financing for Development," chaired by Ernesto Zedillo, 22 June 2001.

2. From a speech by James D. Wolfensohn, "A New Compact to Meet the Challenge of Global Poverty," 14 May 2001, given at the Third Annual Conference on the Parliamentary Network of The World Bank, Berne, Switzerland, <www.worldbank.org>.

3. Paul O'Neill, quoted in Alan Friedman, "UN Lenders Warn of Dangers in Health Gap," *International Herald Tribune,* 4 February 2002, p. 1.

4. For Millennium targets, see a speech by James D. Wolfensohn, "A Partnership for Development and Peace," 6 December 2002, given to the Economics Club of Washington, DC, <www.worldbank.org>.

5. Kofi Annan, speech to the London School of Economics, 25 February 2002.

6. C. K. Prahalad and Stuart L. Hart, "The Fortune at the Bottom of the Pyramid," *Strategy + Business* 26 (January–February 2002): p. 55.

7. "The Challenge of World Poverty," *The Economist,* 19 April 2002, online edition, <www.economist.com>.

8. For figures on trade, see The World Bank, "Global Economic Prospects, 2002," December 2001, <www.worldbank.org>.

9. Estimates for future aid requirements come from United Nations, "Report of the High-Level."

10. For figure that aid is 10 percent lower, see Alan Beattie, "A Measure of Good Intentions," *Financial Times,* 11 March 2002, p. 15.

11. For costs of technical assistance to WTO, see Lael Brainard,

"Ready to Launch: The Prospects for Global Trade Negotiations," *Brookings Review* (Fall 2001): p. 16.

12. George W. Bush, quoted in Joseph Kahn, "Buying Friends or Building Nations?" *New York Times,* 24 March 2002, section 3, p. 5.

13. For background on health, see Jeffrey D. Sachs, chair, "Macroeconomics and Health: Investing in Health for Economic Development," report of the Commission on Macroeconomics and Health, Geneva, Switzerland, 20 December 2001; World Economic Forum, "Global Health Initiative," report of World Economic Forum, New York City, February 2002.

14. Hernando de Soto, "The Constituency of Terror," *New York Times,* 15 October 2001, p. A19.

15. Geoffrey Cowley, "Bill's Biggest Bet Yet," *Newsweek,* 4 February 2002, p. 47.

16. For figures on Islamic nations, see Bernard Hoekman and Patrick Messerlin, "Harnessing Trade for Development and Growth in the Middle East," paper published by the Council on Foreign Relations, New York, February 2002; and David Hale, "The Muslim World, Democracy and Economic Integration," *The Globalist,* 27 March 2002, <www.theglobalist .com/nor/richter/2002/03-27 02.shtml>.

17. Hoekman and Messerlin, "Harnessing Trade."

CHAPTER 9: EXPANDING CORPORATE CITIZENSHIP

1. William Ford, Jr., interview with author, 19 October 1999.

2. For background on social reporting, see Amy Cortese, "The New Accountability: Tracking the Social Costs," *New York Times,* 24 March 2002, section 3, p. 4.

3. Manufacturers Alliance and National Association of Manufacturers, "U.S. Manufacturing Industry's Impact on Ethical, Labor, and Environmental Standards in Developing Countries: A Survey of Current Practices," April 2001.

4. Global Reporting Initiative, "Sustainability Reporting Guidelines on Economic, Environmental, and Social Performance," June 2000, on-line edition, <www.globalreporting.org>.

5. For background on mining codes, see Matthew Jones, "Mining Companies to Seek Minimum Social Standards," *Financial Times,* 30 January 2002, p. 5.

6. Geoff Dyer, "Biotech Sector Urged to Focus on Problems of Poor Countries," *Financial Times,* 12 June 2002, p.8.

7. Roger L. Martin, "The Virtue Martix," *Harvard Business Review,* March 2002, p. 72.

8. Bennett Freeman, "Drilling for Common Ground," *Foreign Policy,* July/August 2001, p. 50.

9. John Browne, speech given at Chatham House, 27 February 2002; and Alison Maitland, "McDonald's Responds to Anti-Capitalist Grilling," *Financial Times,* 15 April 2002, p. 8.

10. For background on trisector cooperation, see Business Partners for Development, "Putting Partnering to Work," <www.bpdweb.org>.

11. Alison Maitland, "Human Rights and Accountability," *Financial Times,* 13 June 2002, online edition, <www.ft.com>.

12. James Gustave Speth, "The Failure of Green Governance," speech at Oxford University, 14 May 2002, to be reprinted in *Foreign Policy* magazine, forthcoming.

CHAPTER 10: INFLUENCING FOREIGN POLICY

1. Serge Schmemann, "A Growing List of Foes Now Suddenly Friends," *New York Times,* 5 October 2001, p. B3.

2. George W. Bush, quoted in Elizabeth Bumiller, "Bush Vows to Aid Other Countries in War on Terror," *New York Times,* 12 March 2002, p. 1.

3. For brutality of what it takes to deal with terrorists, I have drawn on Bruce Hoffman, "A Nasty Business," *Atlantic Monthly,* January 2002, online edition, <www.theatlantic.com>.

4. For discussion of overwhelming American power, I have drawn on Joseph Nye, "The New Rome Meets the New Barbarians," *The Economist,* 21 March 2002, online edition, <www.economist.com>; Paul Kennedy, "The Measure of American Power," *Financial Times,* 2 February 2002, online edition, <www.ft.com>; Gerald Baker, "Nato's Welcome Imbalance in Military Might," *Financial Times,* 7 February 2002, p. 11.

5. For Condoleezza Rice and Richard Haas quotes, see Nicholas Lemann, "The New World Order," *New Yorker,* 25 March 2002, online edition, <www.newyorker.com>.

6. President Bush, in a speech at West Point, 1 June 2002, <www.whitehouse.gov>.

7. Chris Patten, "Jaw-Jaw, Not War-War," *Financial Times,* 15 February 2002, p. 16.

8. Thomas L. Friedman, "The End of Nato?" *New York Times*, 3 February 2002, section 4, p. 15.

9. Christopher Marquis, "For Allies, 'I Do' Becomes 'Hey, Want to Dance?'" *New York Times*, 14 April 2002, section 4, p. 5.

10. Russell Feingold, quoted in Neil A. Lewis, "U.S. Rejects All Support for New Court on Atrocities," *New York Times*, 7 May 2002, p. A11.

11. Dominique Moisi, "Why the U.S. Cannot Defeat Terrorism on Its Own," *Financial Times*, 3 June 2002, p. 13.

12. Todd S. Purdum, "Uzbekistan's Leader Doubts Chances for Afghan Peace," *New York Times*, 14 March 2002, p. A18.

13. Michael Ignatieff, "Is the Human Rights Era Ending?" *New York Times*, 5 February 2002, p. A25.

14. Ahmed Rashid, "Repression Is Rising in Central Asia," *Wall Street Journal*, 13 May 2002, p. A13.

15. Richard C. Holbrooke, quoted in Albert R. Hunt, "An Accelerated Agenda for the Terrorism Threat," *Wall Street Journal*, 25 October 2001, p. A21; and Gallup Poll of the Islamic World, 26 February 2002.

16. Carla A. Hills and Richard C. Holbrooke, "Improving the U.S. Public Diplomacy Campaign in the War against Terrorism," report of the Independent Task Force on America's Response to Terrorism, Council on Foreign Relations, New York, November 2001.

17. See Anthony J. Blinken, "Winning the War of Ideas," *The Washington Quarterly* 25, no. 2 (Spring 2002): p. 110.

18. For background on the White House Coalition Information Center, see Elizabeth Becker and James Dao, "Bush Will Keep the Wartime Operation Promoting America," *New York Times*, 20 February 2002, p. A11.

19. Charlotte Beers, Remarks to the Chief Executive Leadership Institute, Yale School of Management, 30 May 2002, author's notes.

20. Jim Wilkinson, quoted in Miranda Green, "Washington Focuses on Winning Propaganda War," *Financial Times*, 13 March 2002, p. 2.

CHAPTER 11: IMPROVING BUSINESS EDUCATION

1. For background on business education, see the Initiative for Social Innovation through Business at the Aspen Institute; Linda Anderson, "Rivalry? No, It Is Really a Case of Synergy," *Financial Times*, 25 March 2002, Business Education section., p. III.

2. World Resources Institute and Aspen Institute, "Beyond Grey Pinstripes 2001," discussion paper of the World Resources Institute (Washington, DC) and the Aspen Institute (New York), p. 7.

3. Jerold L. Zimmerman, "Can American Business Schools Survive?" Simon School of Business, Financial Research and Policy Working Paper #FR01-16, 5 September 2001.

4. World Resources Institute and Aspen Institute, "Beyond Grey Pinstripes 2001," p. 6.

JEFFREY E. GARTEN is Dean of the Yale School of Management and a columnist for *Business Week*. Formerly a Managing Director of Lehman Brothers Inc. and The Blackstone Group on Wall Street, he also held senior economic and foreign policy positions in the Nixon, Ford, Carter, and Clinton administrations. His articles have appeared in the *New York Times,* the *Wall Street Journal, Foreign Affairs,* and the *Harvard Business Review*. He lives with his wife, Ina, in Connecticut and New York.